The Frolic's Charisma

The Illumination of Seduction, Romance and Passion

By Khalid A. Mustafa

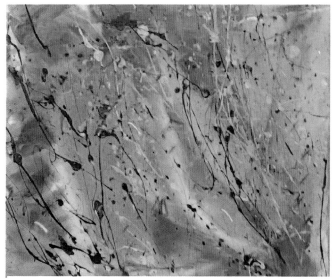

Figure 1 First Stroke - Khalid A. Mustafa

TABLE OF CONTENTS

Printed by MIT Press Bookstore 2017

SUPPLICATION

Al-Islam is a holistic health way of life

 My Lord! The Originator of Creation! Allah! I plead for Your Mercy, Forgiveness and Salvation. Indeed, Your Mercy, Forgiveness and Salvation reigns the heavens and the earth. I prostrate to You for the proper illumination of my soul and smooth entry into Paradise. Oh Allah, pardon my sins and anything I am that transgresses my duty in worship. Establish my feet firmly and help me against those that resist faith. Allow me to lose not heart, nor fall into despair, for I must gain mastery to be true in faith. I seek through Your Guidance health, wealth and solvency. It is my prayer for your Peace and Blessings to be upon the soul of humanity now and forever as Your declaration of justice. Enlighten us with the wisdom of purity of convictions and sincerity of intentions as we sojourn within life. Please allow me to continuously enjoy life, allowing hardships to forge character and wash into the soil of the earth.

PREFACE

To know you is to love you...

Love is a succulent organism seeking a symbiotic relationship towards balancing, acidic and alkaline experiences, our inclinations manifesting as desires. The true nature of eternal love shuns the comfort of blissful ignorance in lieu of tackling difficult challenges with a goal of growth. The way love actively grooves to obtain, it will do to retain. Unless otherwise obstructed love continues reaching for the intensity of passion and joy to remain pure and progressive. The balance of comfort (acidity) and change (alkaline) we yearn is unique, titillating the compatibility we need for a healthy relationship. The Frolic's personality is a playful charismatic flirtation and infatuation stride of love arousing attraction. The mature frolic astutely comprehends that every soul desires autonomy in life, as an individual, but no one really wants to die alone. Our need for independence and companionship forms the complexities of opposing forces only the kindred soul can truly appreciate. Our response, even when we choose to ignore, is a measure of arousal to stimuli that our soul beseechs.

With a breath of life, we arrive unique, possessing a niche of uniqueness no other can claim. Our niche is the passion that moves us forward through the challenges and offers us a vision of success as things fall apart all around us. The passion that illuminates our soul is the greatness within the miracle of our birth. The pleasures in life may seduce us into believing our passions is our passion, diverted from discovering our true purpose I am pointing you to. We can have many passions in life, but we only possess one purposeful passion, that is never discovered in comfort or ease. We must challenge self to investigate the core vibration of our soul, never neglecting the designed role of superficial passions. I advise you as I advise myself that there is a price for greatness and many will plead for you to settle for less. I offer you an opportunity to embrace and excel at the greatness that only you can define. We so often idolize the success of another and neglect to hear the details of their payment. The Frolic's gift is love! A flow of love that blossoms offering nutrients for the soul and seeks expression through intimacy, influenced by the attributes within the particular relationship. As a youth, my intense attraction to beauty was discouraged and I was encouraged to accept the reality of my circumstances. In my attempt to conform to the interpretation pounding my ears and shun the destiny of my soul I discovered the impossibility of denying destiny. I shunned socialization, staying out of the way, living in lethargy, praying to transcend. I suggest you never forfeit your principles, as you read my message with an open mind and learn the lessons of my wisdom. I am truly thankful, for you, allowing me to love you within this prose. There are moments when we must allow our conscience to eat away at our convictions for proper self-awareness. Faith is not an argument, but an evolving state of self. Sharing pleasure and infusing pleasure cultivates very different emotional depth, like the spiritual difference between belief and trust. It is my prayer that I always remain your most treasured discovery, as the foundation for even greater un-expectancies of happiness. Be mindful of worldly ruses and seek to continuously purify your intentions.

I traveled into the depths of purgatory, in search of self, until the impenetrable darkness encompassed my soul and I was thrusted into the light. I paused by the stream's bank, tasting the fish for nourishment and here we are. Witnessing the guidance of my progression I explored my path of defining pure love. The journey of awareness has forged an inspiration of offering my best in the way needed. Unconditional love is a condition of pleasing pleasure for the sole purpose of exquisite pleasure pleasing and guidance towards self-actualization. This realization is at the foundation of a frolic's charisma, as I guide you through seduction, romance and passion Khalid style. My intent is not to be vulgar in words, but to offer you my unadulterated thoughts as a precious value for your mind, heart and soul. The core purpose of my book "The Frolic's Charisma" is to touch the unseen purpose of love that sometimes surfaces as sexual explorations in our life. It is a spiritual journey into physical expression through the moral conscience of your character. When two souls align with kindred dispositions through unique experiences you witness the most sublime intimate expression of love any soul can embrace.

The primal definition for frolic is fun and risqué, full of sensual and seductive play intentionally. The electrifying synergy illuminated is usually considered forbidden, yet alluring as comfort for the soul. The Frolic's life is a voyeuristic exploration of attraction, anticipation, joyfulness, desire and satisfaction. When our natural disposition is balanced with a moral purpose and spiritual guidance you will discover a taste of the most sublime pleasing pleasure possible in human relationships. Of course, to properly benefit you must be what you desire needs. In a conscious intent to let you know my message was not a misprint I emphasize "you must be what you desire needs." It is about a mutual exchange of giving that nourishes the soul and heart of your love. I share the voice of a few who are experiencing my intimate love, as a confirmation of your rightful inheritance. You deserve to be happy and fulfilled with love as you journey the challenges of life with a kindred soul striving for Paradise within sincerity of intentions. The touch is an expression, not the love itself.

I love you in ways I never imagined I could love. How is it that my heart is not exploding in my chest? It is so filled with love for you that it overflows. My love for you, our love, it colors everything I see and feel, every experience, every love. Having you inside me is intoxicating. When you are thrusting inside me, I crave you deeper, harder, there is an edge that I can see and if I allow myself to be free, you carry me over the edge to pleasures that my soul cannot seem to forget.

When you are away, I ache for you, longing for you
to fill me in the way that only you can. Loving me.
Claiming me. Possessing me. Releasing to me. You
and I, we are special in a way that it will be hard for
others to understand. How do we explain
something this deep and passionate and pure?
Something so complete? Something so wonderful
and amazing? I am exhausted by us. Energized by
us. I am blinded. I see more clearly than ever. I am
imprisoned. I am free.

It is advised that each individual needs five
(cheerleader, coach, friend, peer and mentor) in
their life to be truly happy. My journey of love
ignited in the belly of the beast called the Blue
Room and offered a unique perspective in defining
life. The Blue Room is an isolation within isolation
in the darkness of confinement designed to punish
your reasoning of reality. The Blue Room is a form
of torture where restriction is not punishment
enough and you are isolated to battle your demons
in the darkness of a blue light. You are compelled
to discover these five qualities within yourself and

retain your sanity while dancing with insanity. There is no luxury of companionship as the chill of the concrete paralyzes and death awaits wielding its sword. This is the justice of democracy when the absence of intelligence and innocence is taken as arrogance by those in authority. It would be a cute twist of fact to announce my success is merely a state of intellectual prowess, when the fingerprint of divine cradles who I am today. I was born with a passion for moral imagination, intuitively understanding that what feels right and what is right can be distinctly two different realities. I am a servant of the Originator of Creation understood as Allah. With a purposeful mind haunting my impulsive call to purpose I heard the guidance of light in the depths of darkness. The patterns we form as a blueprint of who we are is expressed within the actions of opportunity. Sitting in the center of my four corner room, listening to the rodents search for food, I gave my word that I will keep my word and the light illuminated my heart. In that moment I seduced, romanced and made love to myself as a conscience response.

The acute convergence of lessons in my life possess a value volumes of intellectual considerations wane in measurement. Until you experience the enlightenment offered through sincere intentions and purity of heart I suggest you pause and consider my words carefully before dismissing their purpose. Experience understands what youthfulness (intellectual learning) cannot comprehend of truth, even when it possesses all the data. The nature of youthfulness is to deplete, while the nature of experience is to preserve. The balance is sometimes referred to as obtaining (youthfulness), until we realize the wisdom of retaining the uniqueness that is ours alone to witness. The quality of life is not in how fast and hard we live, but what is actually accomplished as the foundation for the seed to astutely mature. Too often living the life supersedes building a life until dismay arrives in life. I rest here for your review, nourishing the few with value.

When youthfulness and experience aligns the most amazing revelations of love actualize. We are encouraged through media to favor emotional reasoning and feeling what is right instead of considering the deeper implications of language in supporting a cause. It is critical to be mindful that the intent of any media or medium is to control the flow of content towards a specific purpose. The history of our future is a statement of awareness that what we do today will be the history of our future. Within our journey of purpose, as a leader or follower, we taste dimensions of the unseen, knowingly or unknowingly, that offer us a choice. As we gaze through the prism of love we can either embrace the purity of sex (intense physical pleasure), the purity of lovemaking (intense spiritual pleasure) or a sublime balance of the two within this creation of duality, as we glide towards destiny willingly or unwillingly. I purpose, which I am sure you have heard before, that women want to be appreciated and men want to be respected. The real challenge is, can you respect your woman enough to appreciate her and can you appreciate your man enough to respect him? You can pass through life without learning or you can learn while passing through life. I believe appreciation is a form of respect and respect is a form of appreciation that cannot be disconnected in serving a dish of love. The two attribute balance for our foundation within our relationship and we merge as one offering the pleasing pleasure of pleasure pleasing that cannot be experienced otherwise.

I am sure there will be those who object to my vile experiences as pointers towards the wisdom of sacred scriptures and demand a response to who has validated my references. The only scholar you have for truth in the Blue Room is Allah (The All) and the lure of Satan is obvious in the absence of worldly distractions. I ask you would Satan suggest or in my case demand I submit my whole self wholly to the Originator of Creation? We are all familiar with the idea of I think therefore I am and the implications towards human intelligence distinguishing us from other animal life. All we could ever comprehend flows from The Source and we will never comprehend all things of The Source. In our attempt to define everything through what we comprehend limits what is possible to vainness. Whatever attribute we decide to define the Originator of Creation with the key is submission and you will be guided. There is a lesson in my experiences offering value to the reader in a way that is intended to speak to the unique vibration of each soul, while addressing the collective whole in the same breath. Keep your mind open for the chapter "Allah! The All!" where I seduce, romance and make love to you with esoteric insights.

LOVE NOTE

My love,

You are all that I have dreamt of, prayed for, and desired. It is my wish to give the same to you, bringing happiness to your heart's doorstep as you open the door to receive all that is yours. You are my closest confidant and surely my mind, body and soul call you by many names. For so long, I have been alone, waiting for you to share this journey with me. And what is a journey? For some it is simply an excursion, a moving from one place to another. But for us, there is always a deeper meaning. This journey, this passage through the stages of life, we were meant to travel these roads together. I have been stumbling along. My instincts repressed, my sight blinded by lack of truth, searching for salvation while lacking so much knowledge, trust, and faith. I am coming to understand who I truly am and life's true nature. You have pressed upon me the presence of duality and I have accepted that life is defined, in part, by challenge. I am coming to accept this, like the cool breeze after a spring shower or the storm that chases the lightening. I know now that with joy there is pain and I accept that this is a natural occurrence in life, and far different from the infliction of pain. Your love nourishes me and in so many ways, I am yours. Your heart should be at peace, knowing that it is at home with me. Allow me to love you for who you are in all ways and be free with me, knowing that you could never hurt me. If you believe that you inflict pain on those you claim to love the most, then you must not *love me for you could never hurt me. I claimed your love a long time ago and you mine. Stay true to me in your heart and any pain that comes will bring the sweetest scent of happiness.*

There will be many loves in our lives and rare will be the one who understands what we share. The board has been set many times, with all of the players in place and I have followed your moves and set many also, leaving others unaware of the greater plan at play. This is something we much bear individually and together. For my part, my intent was to love you and experience you, never to hurt another, as I sought to embrace Allah by embracing love. It is a difficult thing to deal in truth. It causes some to place blame unfairly an inappropriately, others to throw diversions, and still others to run. It is a difficult thing to deal in truth and while I have not yet perfected the craft, I am committed to seeking this and I would not have anything in its place.

Your life is a blessing to mine and to those who allow you to enter. Knowing you, really knowing you, is to commit to knowing oneself and not all are up to the experience. Live your life authentically and everyone, young and old, will not be able to escape what you lay before them. In everything you do you teach and your focus is centered squarely on the love of the One True God. Stay your course, my love, with Allah, and the Angels will protect you always.

Talent is a powerful Aphrodisiac, delivering pleasure through sensual intelligence, promising to have you all aquiver. A linguistic euphoria of delectable cream and cunnilingus splendor for your senses. Cum for a taste...

Figure 2 Khalid A Mustafa Antique Collectables

PART ONE –

SEDUCTION

HERE I AM

This book encompasses insights about self-love and its influence on how we love others. The intimate relationships we embrace is a reflection of our inner balance of feminine and masculine qualities. How we love touches our need for intimacy and in special relationships our intimacy evolves into sexual expression. It is only through explicit expression and honest communication that we are able to maintain the lust in love through the life of marriage. It is essential to offer all of self in this way, to harmoniously and freely stride into what must be for pleasure. The commitment to sincerity of intentions and purity of communication is the pathway of smooth acceptance through the gates of Paradise. I am sure my mystic companions will appreciate the many layers of meaning in through my words, even as they object to me applying spiritual insights to carnal delights in lust. I often ponder the paradox of when scholars decide when a hardship is defined as a punishment for wrong committed or trial to test your faith. Allah is not shy of the truth, as we ponder to make sense of our purpose.

Stop!

Pause with me for a moment

I can hear my heart beating rapidly to the warmth of your presence

I am drawn towards the aroma of your arousal

Your lips part slightly as I move closer

The pleasing pleasure of pleasure pleasing you exhilarates every nerve

We kiss so lightly, as I nibble on your bottom lip

Tasting the sweetness of your tongue illuminates my passion

Your body melts into mine

I grasp firmly as I gaze into your eyes

The arousal is the guide always in all ways

Blessed passion, baby

Here I am

With each line I script I realize there is still so much more to say as clarification within the multiple paths within seduction and romance. I suspect clarification and justification is needed for the doubtful and truthfully decide my message is for the soul receptive to better. My belief in life after death is not simple a cry for immorality, but an acceptance that life is a journey and not the destination. I muse a reality of oneness where duality is absent and everything possible is all good with the Originator of Creation. We must be mindful of judging an independent creation by the laws of the only creation we know and defining our comprehension as the ultimate truth. I am open to understanding you as we evolve together in this life and redefining what is possible with us every step of the way. In my quest for accurate thinking I must be careful of imposing demands on the free-will of another and master my response for insightful communication. It is not about conforming to my perception of right, but exploring the depths of our common aspirations.

It is my assertion that all negative thoughts are frustrations of positive desires and every adversity carries the seed of equivalent advantage. We must accept our vulnerability to influences on our beliefs, opinions and thoughts, based on the intentions of the source of our consumption. In this way, you will usually discover very different perspectives between those who are blessed to experience and those who gain their understanding through media outlets. The experience offers you a very different perspective than studying the experience. I will admit there are some experiences worth shunning completely, but now they are part of who I am today. There is so much passion I cannot reconcile and am not attempting to justify, as I reveal self in an effort to share the wisdom of my experiences.

The road to opulence beyond palliative is through the gate of definiteness of purpose, mastery of self, learning through adversity, controlling environmental influences (associates), time (giving permanency to positive), harmony and caution (thinking before acting). Harnessing the power of independent thought clothed in definiteness of purpose is the rhythm we need to establish as a habit. The challenge today is that social media technological platforms allow so many covert and overt villains into the heart of our thinking. We bath lavishly in the symptoms of our concern and refuse to address the cause of the contagious disease. Forging the ambition, courage and tenacity to outwit our demon will purge those touched by our life. We must study the curriculum of creation to think accurately with a persistence to understand our human propensity towards evil in designing a solution for good. The blessing of my love is disguised no more, as I arrive unconquered, enlightening your mind with infinite intelligence.

THE HEART IS MINE

Love as life is a paradox within giving to experience the full blessing of the journey. Loving yourself empowers us to love another better and loving another empowers us to love yourself better. Love ignites and nurtures the best within, flowing abundantly upon those we touch. Forgiveness does not exonerate the guilty, but frees your soul from the stain of the pain. I am extending you a breath, in prayer, you will allow my passion for love to be the friendship, kindness, patience, wisdom, intuition, sense of humor, laughter, joy and completeness you yearn. The attributes of character forged into my essence is flourishing with nutrients for your soul. I will attempt to select my words carefully and arrange them properly for the best meaning, but it is the motivations of our intentions that form the relationship. The sincerity of intentions within love is about being intensely authentic through every moment of the caress.

Our sincere intentions must be woven into the tapestry of how we carry ourselves and how we express ourselves, offering more substance than just to woo or coo for the panties. I have never been one of those brothers a woman would hand their number upon seeing, no matter how well-tailored. However, the advantage of earning my way forged a character of substance that flows with my form. When I am on point, after the introduction and in the moment of dead space, I spit a line that extends a volume of content for the mind I am seeking. I glance into her eyes and gaze at her lips as I say "How can a brother get to know you better?" to observe how her lips form to respond. The question searches for an intimate connection beyond the physical attraction of initial interest. It also addresses a subtle fact that women\feminine (womb of mind) choose as men\masculine (mind) pursue. She will appear! The real challenge for the male ego is to swim through the multitudes of rejection in the search of possibility through probability while shunning the insistence of certainty. The impulse is to obtain, gain, contain and possess in our youthfulness. In an instinctive way it is connected to building the legacy we want stamped on our life accomplishments.

I was once an intellectual, studying to validate what I knew in the eyes of another. The idea was to be observed as the monk resting on the mountain top, looking down on the people and isolating myself from the thankless work needing to be done. The lesson I neglected to comprehend in this pursuit, with all that heavy knowledge pounding my brain, is that Prophet Muhammad (SAW) retreated to the cave for Revelation and not as an abode. The paradox of wisdom that ascends from within is for nutritious consumption and practical application, offering itself as armor against the rejection received when in the trenches doing the work. The work that carries little glory in the eyes of others, yet so many claim as their possession. I am the scorn soul pleading to be heard in the silence of the pause between words. I will come, go and leave an impression on your sense of purpose. You will not discover me lingering within the superficial attraction of lust in the way one dresses, carries themselves, the possession of some physical characteristic we visualize as sexy or any bale thrills of temptation. I am the unseen beauty your heart yearns through the carnal explorations you enjoy.

When we offer ourselves to physical attraction we pursue instead of being seduced by the content of character. If the attraction is not equally measured, we either abandon interest all together or abandon teasing with anticipation. The anticipation of receiving or possessing the valuables we sense as desirable becomes the lure and can be flipped to where your presence becomes the lure. We know instinctively that the lure of seduction is in the art of teasing and anticipation. The invitation to taste is always an exploration worth experiencing in solidifying what is possible. It must be astutely understood that the pleasures in sex is not lovemaking to the frolic, even if others use the words interchangeably. Lovemaking's intent is longevity, through the gift of the heart during sexual expression. The masculine prowess of pressure must be in harmony with the feminine prowess of rhythm, shared harmoniously between partners to secrete the elixir yearned to satisfy the heart. I am talking about loving to love in the way that is needed, equally delivered by the transmitter and receiver as a mutual harmonious vibration.

Within the planning of throwing the biggest fundraising party ever in Boston, I pierce through the darkness of the Blue Room and seduced myself into destiny. Images of me dancing with Ms. Wynne entertained my senses, as my spirit rises into leadership as an invisible man. The intensity of my light illuminates within, as others remain oblivious to my presence. I envisioned orchids blooming in the corner of the cell, surrounded by plush grass, as the sun rays reflected in my eyes. The vision of freedom possessed reality and teased the unconscious perception of fact. As the anticipation of success danced on my palate and calm consumed my soul, the orchids blooming across the grass aroused excitement and caressed my forelock. The orchid's ambiance illuminates an aroma reserved to tantalize the deepest and sublime passions known to human experience. Pleasance appeared! Pleasance is an attitude of exquisite beauty exemplified by natural form and forged through meticulous cultivation of the orchid. In tasting the exquisite beauty envisioned through the vibrations of my mind I met Pleasance. Pleasance is the potential of beauty never actualized in the life of a woman. The journey taught me to identify this potential and understand the possibilities when embraced. Your body, heart and soul must work in acute harmony to cultivate exquisite beauty defined in Pleasance.

In my journey of love, I have embraced the potential of pleasance in four specific women and observed how fear veiled their light. The usage of the term love for Plume was off limits in defining our friendship and she dropped this recommendation style acknowledgement:

Khalid's wonderful ability to communicate a diverse viewpoint on a variety of topics is a matter of boundless wonder. Conversations stay lively and mind expanding. He is a dedicated and reliable friend with significant talent. His continual pursuit of personal endeavors and career successes have allowed him to make invaluable contributions to the community. His accomplishments are pure hard work and consistency without limitations.

Of course, I see true friendship as a flavor of love, in contrast to merely being long time acquaintances. I am always interested in understanding the motivation in running from love in a platonic friendship, as if the thought itself is a sin. I surmise there is an anticipated, unwanted expectation, implied in the word that motivates us to keep our distance. The complications and complexities in human relationships are diverse and unique. The distance formed within complications and complexities motivates me to seek understanding. Understanding allows me to properly respect the boundary and clarify the direction of my journey in the friendship. In the same way, there are flavors of love when we decide to be intimate, there are many flavors of intimacy. The sharing of something very personal is a flavor of intimacy, just as a physical embrace is a flavor of intimacy. The inclination of a frolic is to flirt with intimacy to explore the possibilities.

The forth Pleasance, Vanilla Pleasance, exemplified more than anyone the influence of deception in forming character. She continuously hides self from herself and especially from others as a protection. I pursued into the depths of her soul to discover a heart waiting for my arrival. We acknowledge our gift awarded the other, through the intimacy and caring shared across challenges attempting to abort destiny. We are incompatible in so many fundamental ways, but circumstances bonded us in a sensual way. Our friendship extended an opportunity to unlock the deceptions supporting the foundational perceptions in our life. She is actually a very different person beneath the persona, hiding from herself in so many ways. It is an amazing journey of loving an incompatible opposite for the purity of the experience, through meticulous cultivation. Her presence guided me into the light of a social life by default and still there is so much potential that will never be. Vanilla Pleasance exemplifies why people are never as they appear on the surface, to protect the essence blessing them with life. Each vanishing Pleasance guided me to a more rewarding love I define as Berry on the path for Blossom. You will hear your voice in my prose as you sense the vibrations of love through the words of women offering me the most exquisite aphrodisiacs enthralling the heart.

The clinking of the keys thrusted me into the present and still the vision (Blossom) of walking down the street shaking hands and hugging admirers was real. Once you become enthralled with the intensity of the passion caressing your soul you instantly acknowledge dissatisfactions and must decide to become better or bitter. Better instead of bitter was my mantra from that moment forward and my life bears testimony. Even as I romanced myself, with the gifts of experiences, it was essential to continuously and consistently seduce myself. We were taught and conditioned, in the sixties, that embracing passions is mischievous at best. We were advised to deny, run away from or ignore these cooing sensations and conform. The love deepened with each passing moment and this time the clinging led to the door opening. What I expect from myself always out pace any expectation of another and this has been accepted as conformity. Profanity ceased being the suffix, verb and prefix of my sentence structure to an occasional expression for impact. There is a calm in the center of every violently raging storm know to some as opportunity. I took the opportunity and here I am in print for eternity. This script is the opening and life after death revelation of truth, as a hint to the wise.

In transforming my own way of thinking I realized my purpose to live and I was determined to prove my current destiny wrong. The consideration of nurturing intangible human qualities into tangible values with savvy charisma amused my consciousness. Through the blessings of my unique circumstances I took a step into change and the attitude changed how I perceived experiences influencing my behavior. The layers of doubt, as the distractions consumed me, rested on my palate when I was blessed to study the renowned scholars. The pursuit of intimate expression was proclaimed sinful and I was advised to shun what was revealed to my soul. In my earnest attempt to conform to conventional religious thought led to unhappiness, confusion and punishment. I discarded the distraction of their interpretation of sacred scripture and decided to study revelation through creation. It was foolish to allow myself to be seduced by the interpretation of another that did not even acknowledge my reality. My essence guided me towards a social entrepreneurship of moral conscience, which will speak to the essence of your character and caress your innate uniqueness. I love to love! I advise you as I advise myself, enlightenment usually arrives in the most unorthodox way, as a means of testing the purity of our intentions. When you cultivate the necessary trust and confidence transformation commences a piercing towards pleasance.

I became the beacon of opportunity to change the way others thought about me and about themselves through the way I responded to challenges, suppression or oppression. The illumination of my core purpose and talent of love became self-evident. The transformation guided me into roles as an educator and my success as an educator guided me into roles of leadership. I rose from the ashes of the concrete jungle to emerge as an anchor for possibility. I was ready to die! When I think back over the years of my life it feels like a have lived five lives and stepped squarely into spiritual awareness. I elevated my consciousness beyond what is defined as the alpha man and embraced the sensitivities of my Y Chromosome as a masculine attribute. I am sure in today's sexual environment this statement will be grossly misunderstood, but I must accept that risk in order to resonate your frequency. I am intentionally stimulating your ability to identify hearts that naturally harmonize with you. It is an element of stimulation in the Art of Emotional Polarity, embedded in the laws of the universe. I doubt even dedicating a chapter to this conversation will do the subject justice, as I deposit gems for you to barter with in the future. I have looked evil in the eye and we played Russian roulette in the depths of darkness.

It may appear I have slid of topic in part three of this book, yet it is the lessons within the primal principles of lust we must listen to. I am the sum total of my experiences, far removed from pure on my journey to the Gates of Paradise. The idea, in my personalized journey, is to unpack all that is impure and approach the gate pristine. I do not expect or anticipate many to be on this road with me, as I rise as an individual soul. The seed of sincerity in intentions is at the core of all principles of success offering us a prism of approaches on one path to The Source. Wisdom is the definitive act of aligning thoughts harmoniously with universal laws to form a progressive state of consciousness unwaveringly committed to your goal. I understand, acknowledging the theme of Ralph Ellison's The Invisible Man, that despite how much light I illuminate I will remain invisible to the majority. The legacy of my opulence rest in how I am received through the words of this prose and what you are willing to invest. In mentioning invest I cannot leave this paragraph without mentioning this change agent in the math for your consideration. If a million individuals reserved a mere ten dollars, in a week, to invest one dollar towards ten individuals we would literally create ten millionaires a week. With each millionaire investing ten dollars a week to ten individuals our millionaire production will compound and shift the paradigm of wealth. I emphasize invest and not donate or give. We are conditioned through the medium of public media to support individuals who do not have our best interest at heart and we neglect to even identify individuals in our community worthy of our support. Individuals who have already sacrificed fame and fortune for the cause. I make honorable mention of the Syracuse 8, while we all embrace and rejoice in the knee taken by Mr. Colin Kaepernick. Supporting the best in us is the key to substantial and lasting success.

When my sensitivities of love cooed the ears of women it inspired a fresh flavor of expression for success. The sexy eye contact, girlish smile and the consistent stepping into my space where clues of attraction I did not recognize. I was oblivious, until they bathed me into awareness and groomed my sensitivities. Applying the correct pressure, through asking the right questions, removed inhibitions. I mastered the playful touch as I listened to the details of your marriages, lovers, desires and fears. I understand your sense of self better than the men you have been sleeping with for years. In the rare occasions where sexual innuendos emanate from the chemistry of our connection you should never fear sex is inevitable. Khalid, as any unadulterated frolic, does not ascribe to the art of sex independent of love making. The unadulterated frolic is a sublime lover and caresses a bond that never evaporates with time or distance. Our dance is not a lesson in what a man can obtain, but what is retained once you are smitten and uncontrollably lean in for the first kiss. I inhale the aroma rising through relieving your pain and releasing a storm of sweet, sticky juices flowing between your thighs.

I can hear your heart and yearning of your soul within a glance. It is the courageous few who are ready and willing to step into the darkness of the light to claim victory. It is suggested that a content heart cannot be seduced, as time changes where we are. Content implies an absence of ambition for better. It is a balance of attraction, compatibility and communication that continuously matures the relationship towards true contentment as a destination never achieved. You must keep your eye on the prize and that mandates careful attention within every step. When the rituals or patterns in our relationship causes neglect of appreciation and absence of respect you are on a content decline and primed for love frolic style. The continuous nurturing communication, with the patience to hear, is critical in every intimate relationship. Your intention, prayer and action must be aligned with purpose of desire to enjoy the presence of who a person needs to be. The reality is that everything is connected for a reason and must be acted on as a continuum of circumstances leading towards a very specific experience of overwhelming joy. You must know me to love me. I am the scepter of your province in the rhythm of our dance.

THE SCIENCE OF SEDUCTIVE ATTRACTION

We know the love or lack of love from parents, siblings, relatives and friends in some form or another. However, we rarely explore what these relationships mean for the self-actualization of our soul. We must be willing to ask why and approach the conversation to dispute assumptions, in defining romantic love and passionate lust. You must be able to discern between the two and know the blessing of both before they merge into lovemaking. Within the journey we must explore what we sense as our core purpose and listen to the harmony of our heartbeat, as our soul's illuminate as one light. We can look beyond urging hormones motivating action and consider the real touch of love. It is not my intent to suggest I have all the answers, but to extend my insight as a guide towards your uniqueness. I will awaken your passion with ideas that presently allude your comprehension and entice you to ask questions of yourself. It is not about being the answer, but offering the guidance for you to live life consciously conscience. Believe me, I have more issues than Time magazine and still I rise. The joy of living fully and embracing risk is my courage to move towards self-actualization and is my encouragement to sacrifice for better.

Attraction in the form of seduction is lustful and alluring. Lust is the flavor of attraction that is motivated by intense carnal desire in absence of sensing anything about the soul of the person. Allurement is the flavor of subtle attraction through the sense of energy exchange. Allurement is cultivated over time where lust is instantaneous. Both flavors of attraction are unconscious manifestations of the subconscious energy alignment of what we think (belief) and feel. The true purpose of prayer or supplication, through my observation, is to ask as we demand an answer for what we truly believe and feel is our innate inheritance. When the universe responds favorable to what we think and feel it acts as an absolute confirmation to what is. The chemistry we share is an influence of the biological temperament and experiences of who we are identifying as a mate. The chemistry formula is true of all relationship mating and is not exclusive to sexual mating compatibility. Our sexual interest arrives in the form of flirting in a way to suggest sexual attraction. The attraction, romantic cooing and deep attachment is fundamental for all intimate relationships. The decision for sexual expression is a conscience sense of self and yearning for physical connection in the process of completeness.

There is a natural anticipation that is cultivated as any relationship is formed and each person becomes comfortable with the others' essence of existence. Spoken and implied commitments contribute fuel towards the emotional bond and intensifies our anticipation. When you connect sentimental sensitivities with character compatibilities, in any relationship, you stimulate electrifying passions that yearn to be satisfied. Anticipation continues to flourish through the continuum of experiences and information gained on the journey towards the summit of destiny. Our anticipation forces us to review the details in more detail, looking for the signs that will confirm our intentions. Each day we test the boundaries of our understanding to make sure we are moving in the correct direction. When we challenge our conscience to offer a finite decision it excites our sensitivities of right and wrong, as we justify our feelings through information defined as fact. The seducer must be seduced in order for the attraction to be genuine in an intimate exploration of passion. The seduced must know their attribute of seduction in order for the attraction to be more than lust. The seducer should never confuse lust or even the love of lust as love.

Love is truly an essential emotional, moral and spiritual journey towards maturity to grasp happiness. Unadulterated love is an indescribable pleasing pleasure only known through experience that flings the gates of bliss open in the Hereafter in anticipation of your arrival. If you grasp too firmly to the physical relationship you will deny yourself proper self-actualization. Every validated religious scripture I have ever studied clearly emphasizes the determining factor of sincerity and destiny in each decision. When we cling to the physical over listening to the heartbeat of our soul an injustice is committed upon the sincerity of our intentions. Every mind must tend to the vibrations of its own destiny. It is about having the courage to risk good for great and never having cause to regret the journey. Once your heart identifies your sincerity of intention as the guidepost, you will possess the courage to respond. The journey towards pleasing pleasure is an act of maturity that it will guide you towards the intimacy your soul yearns. The science of seduction is understood through explorations nurturing a vision recognizing the unique values within. Yes, there is an emerging darkness that will intensify to the balance of light you seek. It is critical to understand that purging will touch those who are the closest to you. We must trust, having the courage to embrace the future, to move beyond our comfort zone to enjoy the most intensified passions boiling deep within our heart, mind and soul.

I desire for you to learn your distinctive competency of love more than any other soul in the world. As Louis Pasteur stated long ago "fortune favors the prepared mind." Without trust there is no risk-taking and without risk-taking there is no innovation and without innovation there is no progress. Innovation creates a value for problem solving and nurtures creative solutions. If you are comfortable within the good life you have forged I advise you to pause reading and pass this book forward to one having a passion towards a fulfilling life. Creative solutions are dependent on our talent, the foundation we stand on and what we are willing to invest. We are discussing the investment of your heart to commence the most exquisite love ever in the exploration of life. As George Millar once stated, "Education is a process, not a place." However, development is a voluntary process of brutally looking honestly at your strengths and weaknesses. You must become what you desire yearns. It starts with introspection from a positive decision to indulge into what is best for your soul.

Change is doing something different in a consistent way to form a new pattern of vibration. Seduction is a pattern of loving enthusiastically, expressing the beauty of creativity, feeling comfortable with self and embracing the joy of life. It is important to think forward and inwardly instead of outwardly and backwards. The more self-confidence you have, through earnest introspection, the more it diminishes your fears, mythologies and complexities in your mind hindering progress. In the middle of every difficulty lies opportunity and the only question open for debate is whether you trust yourself enough to take advantage of the opportunity or remain a victim to what others might think. We can be what another needs and ignore what we need for sublime happiness. Sexual pleasure should be a natural revelation and not a designed goal in seduction for the charismatic lover or you will forfeit the real gift fueling your possession.

I hear feminine voices musing the scarcity of a good man and understand their concern. Even though statistically more males are born than females, men have a higher risk of death in childhood and as adults. Women fantasize of embracing his satisfying love at the sacrifice of everything, only to end up with a shell of the desired goal at best. She must not only have the courage to embrace her man, but the tactical insight, creative instinct and artistic flair to secure his heart. Otherwise, you're perceived inadequacies will create a self-fulfilling destiny of never securing your possession. The frustration will erode the role of a man and influence your perception of masculinity. When you couple this attack with the warped perception of masculinity by males we have an epidemic on our doorstep. In other words, you will be of the blessed minority to discover, embrace and possess the love that is your birth right. Opportunity is created within every intentional act or response to the plea of our soul. You must be willing to participate in the dance of trust that will metamorphose your personal development and maturity as a woman. Allow me to claim what is properly mine and you will unleash the paradigm of your true value, while experiencing the apex of your most burning yearnings in the same breath.

It still amazes me how we are so deeply hurt by the truth and bathe joyously in a lie. Hesitation or doubt is a tool of fear to keep us within a comfort zone and prevents any real growth. Ideologies that deplete trust and erode the natural evolution of humanity is disguised as our individual right. It is our individual right to decide what is best, yet too often what we claim aligns with the norms of our environment. The reflective mind never stops questioning why they feel or believe a particular way, constantly seeking to understand. We can decide as we please and It will not deplete the role of copulation between male (sperm) and female (egg), in the perpetuation of humanity in this creation of duality. Our individual aspirations should illuminate the nobility of life instead of a selfish "ism" of accumulation. There is duality in darkness, just as there is duality in light. The two opposites, each form a pair that doubles through segmentation. There is a logical justification in the algorithm of a Byte resting as infinity. The true art of seduction respects the rhythm of creation instead of manipulating vulnerabilities through intellectual persuasion built on deceptive assumptions. Seduction seduces the seducer as a guidepost for the seduction. It is natural for the seductress (since seduction of the heart is a feminine quality) to be seduced first. The attraction is the enticement and aphrodisiac to engage. The seductor aims to seduce the mind and the seductress aims to seduce the heart. My intent is to evolve the exquisite beauty within you, even when it thrust you into the arms of another.

I am born to love purely, passionately and instinctively requesting your most cherished quality. It is my way to reveal you to you, with your explicit consent. I am not talking to you as male or even as man, but as the life source pumping your heart. I acquiesce that there are a multitude of intellectual justifications for your unwillingness to taste me and shun the titillation of my freedom. I assure you all else is a palliative and is not the cure your soul yearns. Leaving the comfort of good for great is the price for balance of the most explosive intimate expression of self. I am the forbidden fruit nudging you into freedom of expression and destroying the bond of all false relationships. I am not male, but I am man when your mind is ready. This book is not for the coward, lacking moral courage, clinging desperately to relationships consuming the life from the essence of your heart of hearts and denying you my love.

I mean to inspire connotation with flamboyant mannerism and courage without the recklessness of undisciplined skills. There is an intense power in knowing you can attract or seduce and even a greater power in extending freedom to your possession. You will hear me repeat these words often that unconditional love is a condition. Most of us wander through life with a plethora of unsatisfied needs and we crave a way to be superior or demonstrate our superiority. We observe this pattern, within every relationship, as each of us wield influence and most of us never feel secure enough to extend freedom from our emotional bondage. These pages will guide you, with deep spiritual insight, through exquisite love into wild excursions of intensely sensual explorations. Temptation is not only a lure into doubt, deception and disobedience, but offers us an opportunity to sooth natural desires unique to every individual. We cannot deny the inevitability of temptation and must explore moral means of expression to balance the burning passions of selfish pleasures. Throughout the history of humankind, evoking the spiritual harmony, moral purification and mental equilibrium of love is declared as the wakening or self-realization in the pure worship of the Originator of Creation.

INTIMACY MATURATION

The maturation of intimacy towards the pleasing pleasure of everlasting love is nurtured through physical beauty, mental equilibrium, emotional sensibility, moral purification and spiritual harmony. My eyes gaze upon you and your alluring call stimulates interest. I approach, without hesitation, with an air of purpose. Holding my gaze and focused on your lips I ask, "What does a brother need to do to get to know you?" The silence is a welcomed pause, knowing she is considering you worthy of her attention. My approach cuts to the heart of seduction in knowing her selection has happened long before this moment in time. The astute woman, I am in search of, answers with the question of why would I want to know her. I smile, the dance has begun and my words flows smoothly. I would love to learn if we can offer each other a value no one else has touched. You cannot seduce a complacent, content or jaded heart and so we stand in a moment of truth. Her lips and eyes take form, before another word is spoken, as if she is about to taste something delicious. It is the affirmative answer, as I wait to learn how courageous her words will be. I am swooned by courageous beauty searching for completeness.

The depths and breadth of my willingness to love is eternal and infinitely gracious. Love forges a complicated web of connectivity challenging the boundaries set in circumstances. When I gaze into your eyes I am reminded of why "Us" had to be and why we are incomplete without the other. I enjoy the miracle of possession with a soul who I can be myself with, values my presence, listens to my heart beat and supports the best in me. When I am in your presence possibilities are probable and probabilities a certainty. Just as our love the Arabic time adverb "when" modifies everything except a noun and is certain to be. The implications in this observation is just amazing in understanding that changes happen through activity of the object and not just because the object exist. This is why everyone is initiatively motivated to influence action and we seek to discover this harmony within the aura of another. The connection of our mind, heart and soul only infuses the beauty I taste in the delight of your body. There will never be another who will appreciate you more than me and I will make sure of that by continuously raising the expectation of what we share. I will continuously seduce you through the deepening depth and expanding breadth of sacred love.

Excuse the pause as I remind you that this prose is not about one night stands or superficial excitement that fades after the initial taste of the nectar. Also, this book is not about sex or the usual mating rituals that you can read in a thousand other places. It is about exploring the unconditional condition of love Frolic style. On the path you will discover a multitude of applications and what you embrace is absolutely a personal decision. When you neglect to decide someone else will decide for you and that could be precisely what is needed in the moment. There will also be a moment where you must decide in order to even know the experience is possible. It is not always possible to control what happens to us, but we can control how we respond and that influences what happens to us. We can only respond to opportunity. The sperm released through masturbation is deprived of the fallopian tube mating opportunity and this changes what is possible.

I believe there are primarily two forms of irresistibility we must consider in seduction. The first I will call superficial irresistibility. It is in the way a woman maintains and displays her physical beauty. A posture is formed where you can recognize her in a crowd, where the way she dresses accents what she is looking for in the moment. Every accent possesses duality and the challenge for the male is to understanding the flow to create the harmony in the dance. We can dress for self in the morning, yet the intelligent mind knows dress influences how observers perceive us. The seduced seducer hears the message and reveals the correct key unleashing the moment. Yes, both the superficial irresistibility and superficial excitement can be the seduction into the intimate excitement and/or irresistibility our soul really yearns. The guide towards irresistibility, to stay on topic, is within the seductions intent and is qualified by attitude. The refined bad-boy good-man male needs to connect with the intent of the woman seducing him to experience accurate irresistibility. The act of proof is in the ingredients and not simply the curb appeal. The correctly blended ingredients solidify the bond in the progression of attraction.

The seduction in the art of attraction starts with eye contact and her willingness to face you. I am often more afraid of what will happen instead of what will not. Upon approach the man must then take a second look at the physical form originally getting his attention. We observe how the way she dresses compliment her feet, legs, stomach, ass, back and breast. Her posture is the display of what she thinks of herself as a sexual lure. When the man approaches her aroma starts to stimulate other senses and then he is greeted with a calmly seductive voice inviting him closer. The primal instinct in man to chase, capture, conquer and devour can be satisfied in different forms. Of course, this depends on the disposition of the male. In other words, the process towards irresistibility and within the seduction or attraction process must be reciprocated in the dance by the female for true success. The mind must look beyond what the woman is looking to experience in the moment and hear the heartbeat of her soul to seduce the heart. The male can always overpower the female with intellectual prowess and that can be charming when applicable. Of course, the seduction of the heart is in observing her pace slow and order for your natural stride to catch her.

I was sitting on the corner of East Trade Street observing a sister sitting with her head down. Her body language expressed melancholy at best and I was focused on sensing her sense of self. A young physically fit brother, with his upper torso fully tattooed, was jogging in place at the light in front of her. Impulsively she got up and walked over to him. I could not hear what she said, but he paused jogging in place to respond. The light changed and he jogged across the street. The sister stood there with a childish grin of pleasure and embarrassment on her face. She started to grip her thighs together and sway slightly as if to control the juices flowing from her pearl. It was a prime example of superficial irresistibility in the art of seduction. I will never know why this moment did not lead to an exploration of compatibility, seeing she was brave enough to pass the first word and step into his space to open the opportunity of conversation. They were standing, paused in the moment of offering herself, as she looked him directly in the eye waiting for a touch. I could hear her willingness without a spoken word. I concluded she did not ask for advice, but only passed a soft compliment. I mention this moment for us to consider possibilities within seduction and consider the influences preventing success. The observation implied expectations that were not mutually shared and the prize jogged away. However, the exchange clearing moved her beyond the condition of melancholy and that offered its own reward.

Was the jogger interested or just being respectful? Was the sister interested or just instinctively reaching beyond her current sense of self? The rhetorical sense of these two questions guides us to the factors for irresistibility. Our spiritual, moral and intellectual sensibilities can be stimulated without motivating action. Irresistibility must be dressed with compatibility and interest as the proper expression of the connection. The irresistibility of compatibility and interest her words offer flows from spiritual stimulation through the physical expression of seduction. However, there is a major difference in attitude when a woman is doing what you like because she understands what you like and a woman is doing what she loves and you love it. The culture or character of your relationship is forged through intentions. When two or more individuals can align intentions we possess a mutually beneficial love. As time proceeds, our intention will shift in ways so subtle we may neglect to even consider as important. She will appear, but there is no just appearing that remains when we are blind to critical influences that will destroy the purity of possibilities.

 The reality is the woman must choose you above all the game you can spit and things you can provide or you will be taken in the end. The answer is within the pattern and not the act. We now approach the final flare of true irresistibility when everything else is in place. Intrigue! The woman must not be afraid to evolve naturally and experiment with pleasing pleasure. She must trust the deepest depths of her heart and always explore ways to allow her lover closer. Trust is the ultimate form of respect where all other forms of respect flow. The man must seek delights beyond the happiness of her silence, the food she supplies for his hunger and the sex offered to calm his horniness. He must listen to the vibration of her soul and embrace the passion in her heart. I am a firm believer in the fact that no matter how well you know a person there is always something you need to learn as you grow together. Trust me in this, my brothers, if you are not learning new subtle attributes in your woman you are absolutely growing apart and opening the pathway for alternate sources to sooth her soul.

Our cognitive perception moves us towards a destiny of thought and even false memories to justify belief. What we end up believing over time is usually very different from what actually happened and this maintains our equilibrium of identity when shunning change. It is possible to maintain a long lasting relationship within this illusion and without never ever knowing great in place of good. I submit that good is great for the average person and caution you to carefully consider what you will risk or even destroy in the pursuit of the alluring scent of pleasing pleasure. You will discover honest communication at the center of every healthy relationship, instead of the silence at the center of complacency or the arguing at the apex in a moment of dissatisfaction. It is really not about determining solutions, even though solutions will rise naturally. I find that the willingness to explore the many variations without judgment nurtures a sense of safety for our most vulnerable self. Our worldly interest influences us to focus on blame and winning or someone being wrong as measurements of success. Within a truly intimate relationship eradicating blame, naturalizing wrong and redefining a win while embracing a continuum of what is needed forms lasting fulfillment.

The era of the day is what I will call moral imbecility. Moral imbecility is when your idea of what is morally right does not align with mine and one of us is considered an imbecile by the other. The narrative of your reality is considered truth and the narrative of my reality is considered falsehood. The irony, in this era, is how the most destructive ideas, eloquently articulated, dominate as truth and the balance is treated as imbeciles. Universal truth cradles the biological principles of procreation and our social life is a reflection or perception of this foundation, despite what we are able to manufacture in our mind. The movement declaring the Originator of Creation as omnipotent is stagnated by the roar of the subconscious mind extended to us in "The Secret" and other mystical life coaches. I am not dismissing the validity of their wisdom, only the absoluteness of their understanding. The change sounds glorious, as the mind as a deity, until you consider the implications instead of accepting Allah as The All. I am mostly concerned with limiting the Originator of Creation to the laws of creation or to what our minds can perceive. Our thinking has already evolved from our three-dimension reality to a seven-dimension reality and now the scholars are discussing an eleven-dimension reality. How do we define what we cannot perceive and at what point do we demand cognitive submission?

LURE ME

The natural progression of human life is maturity, while continuously embracing youthfulness to deepening our understanding of love. When observing the behavioral patterns in the inherent structure within the nature of every element in creation I understand how we can conceive the Originator of Creation as change or what I would qualify as The Change. We spiritually comprehend that the Originator of Creation must be independent of creation, in the balance of decay we witness. The lure to define Allah through our perception is rationale, but in no way complete to the morally conscious. Our human essence is evolving towards progression through decay. The irony of the paradox in duality is that we must decay in some form in order to progress in another. We sacrifice for love often, even when it is selfish. Our attraction to the light of love can devour the light of love to offer birth of a truly unique love. What is practical, ethical and intelligent submits to what is sound for the soul. It is in the way we love self, beyond merely loving self, that defines personality types and the way we understand guidance.

The lure of love influences us to grow harmoniously, grow apart or even become stagnant within a relationship. The lure tapestry is in learning, respecting and appreciating the expression of growth within love or we justify with what should be. Our behavior is influenced by our attitude and our attitude influenced by belief. The challenge is believing and forging the courage to embrace the journey. The woo proof ingredients is the presence of play and your comfortability of exposing yourself in the process of honest communication. I take love and pleasure seriously, as I master the foundation of my purpose. I will not be the same person you meet tomorrow as I am today. I consider routine a form of death and discipline a form of life. Routine is when the spontaneous quickie, causing us to be late for work, is replaced by the consistency of the good day kiss. The lure of love should retain its importance minimally equal to our pursuit of materialistic success. However, in this world of deception how people see us is much more important than what is.

Our attribute of certainty infuses the courage of walking with faith and blinds us to the probability of perception and shuns the risk of possibility. When you elevate the value of possibility in the heart of love you construct a foundation very few can compete with as a lure. The deliberate action is to become what my desire needs for true frequency harmony or compatibility to emerge within the art of attraction. The result of our potential depends on the action we take and the action we take is forged through belief or tone of certainty. Change is the creation of the Originator of Creation and change is considered an attribute, but not necessarily an absolute definition of omnipotence. I am reminded of how my physical presence is an attribute of how others perceive who I am, but it is not truly who I am.

In the dance of nurturing intimate relationships, we send out signals to harmonize with the frequency of another in many different forms. However, here are some common insights and ideas for you to consider:

1.   The contended person is almost impossible to seduce

2.   The jaded heart is almost impossible to seduce

3.   Offer the art passion\heat to the lure of a cold heart caress love

4.   You cannot change the foundational condition of another

5.   The nature of love is to give

Yes, we all can be seduced given the correct circumstances and moment of opportunity. With a contended and jaded person, we are satisfied with the way things are and closed to change. The lean towards the safety of beneficial possibilities is not receptive to adventures or risk for better. The efficient predictability of the circumstances or expectations can wear like a comfortable sweater. However, the most efficient is rarely the most progressive or what is best for the balance our heart yearns. Securing a good life can lead us to the safety of prostrating our spirit, heart and mind in quicksand in exchange for security. Our focus of living the life dominates us truly building a life. When our soul, heart or mind is ready for better we instinctively know the power within seduction and probability guides us into the possibility of love. The ability to seduce flows naturally and is a process that starts from within, influencing how we view self and what is possible for our life.

The two forms of seduction are the feminine use of appearances and the masculine use of language. A blend of qualities suggests depth in your uniqueness, which fascinates even as it confuses the receiver. The theatrical streak in leveraging both embodies fantasy and forbidden pleasures. As we are showered with these forbidden tantalizations, we immediately feel innocent and yearn to learn. The theatrical and innocence dance to create an undeniable euphoria within a sense of danger. Intense desire illuminates as a distracting power and thrust towards building the crucial bond of trust. The receiver and transmitter must feel safe in the exchange. Each must be willing to give totally, trusting first, to the seduction. The paradox of life as is love is rooted in the debate of who is the true provider or the lure determining gender, where the principle remains consistent even as the language changes. Biologically, the male provides the sexual chromosome that determines gender and consequently the lure of the ova frequency determines what chromosome is received at the moment of fertility.

Sexual Mental Emulation is the seductive romance in making love where you place yourself in the role of your partner to truly embrace their appetite, fantasies and aspirations. It sounds irrational at first glance, but is dangerously seductive as a charming characteristic. Trusting lovers must circumvent the self-protective process, retaining the playful, receptive spirit of youthfulness to truly be lovers. Defensiveness is deadly in the art of seduction and you must emulate what is desired to guide the relationship. Discretion is always a priority in a healthy relationship. A healthy mind always respects and appreciates discretion. The royal road to seduction is in revealing your vulnerability and helplessness, because the seducer must first be seduced. Offering a glimpse of the firm foundation you are willing to share in love builds trust. You must earn trust or the trust you receive is the property of another and her heart cannot be yours.

Frolic lovers are drawn to offer their heart to those who expect a lot out of life and especially to those willing to accept nothing less than the possession of your heart. The lure in overt independence governed by the willingness to give possesses has a provocative effect, making a statement of challenge and appealing to passion simultaneously. We are not talking about playing hard to get as a challenge, but by illuminating the quality expectations in character. The passions stimulated are seldomly sexual at first glance, searching for a deeper connection that bonds for life. The connections that swiftly moves away from the unfamiliarity of acquaintance and builds friendship is the love expectation. Love is a very influential four letter word, some of us envision as profanity in "I would love to fuck you". We are conditioned to diligently shun the lure or envisage as a naughty release exchange touching the body. The merging of our bodies supplements the merging of our souls, promised by the heart through marriage. Marriage is a sacred institution intended to symbolize, honor and protect this oath of the bond. The commitment should be more than just a safe haven to raise children or a means of financial security. We can accomplish both and much more standing on the same foundation and directed towards our unified purpose. The value of life is diluted when a mind obtains the world while corrupting the soul, sensing our legacy of material gain will offer us immortality.

Within the needy opposites attract, where pure love seeks balance as a healthy formula for success. It is the content of your character that presents the challenge and must be genuine for enduring relationships that extend beyond time and space. You must be patient in allowing your presence to illuminate from within the receiver's heart. Do not be distracted by the receiver's initial exterior of disinterest, anger or retreat. Allow the receiver time to digest the nutrients of your charm feeding their repressed or denied passions. When the pomegranate to ripen and fall it is ripe and at its peak of sweetness. Keep in mind that your selection in seduction is an expression of the receiver subconsciously seducing you.

All things are possible within seduction when you have the time and the circumstances align to present opportunity. The content or complacent heart requires heat to warm its soul and cultivate the ideal environment for seduction, while the projection of desperation distorts the essence of your vibration and causes one to flow into turbulent relationships. In some societies, to marry the youth at the initial signs of romantic interest is to prevent desperation from dominating the decision process in selection. The perceptive eye can filter through the desperation and observe the original beat of the heart. However, a soul swimming in emotional neglect, through the lack of romance and sexual actualization over the years, can be very deceptive. Relationships that seemed to be made in heaven come to a crashing disaster when the deception can be no more. Of course, there is the needy soul, committed to the relationship, who will pretend and grasp intellectual justifications to maintain the relationship for very honorable reasons. I am not trying to position one course of action as better than the other, but to present the differences in the way we decide what is best.

A soul in a committed relationship feeds the possession and that possession becomes the purpose, decaying desires yearning more. We are obligated to check our appetites with wisdom, but must also check the intentions of our education resources. The evil embedded within technology is the exposure to digitalized temptations otherwise never imagined and designed purely for entertainment or more accurately the accumulation of capital on the moral slaughtering of the populace. Our appetites are being tempted from every angle and luring us into a perception of a reality that is vile. It is in the way we approach or neglect to approach digitalized temptations that is cheating our heart of pure happiness. If nothing else is a sign of the ailing human relationship it is found in the bizarre demand for pop-up partners globally. I am not sure how a synthetic doll can offer pleasure, even when you find release. Romance is a lure dance best served through open and direct communication, in our quest for pleasing pleasure with your partner. The release can be the sum total of what we need in avoiding the complications of sexually intimate human relationships. What is acceptable with one is totally unacceptable with another and here we are.

Your mere presence must insinuate what is needed to truly be desired. I advise that no seduction can mature without temptation, excitement and risk. There must be constant tension and suspense that nothing is predictable and everything is possible. The theatrical presence must be articulated through flattery aimed directly at the receiver's insecurities. Affirmation is simply the making of strong positive statements without hesitation. The mind is infinitely vulnerable to suggestion, especially when powerful desires are involved.

Discover what she has never received and you have the ingredients for a deep-rooted seduction. Seduction can offer you exactly what you intended in the most unexpected way. Unconditional love is rare and hard to find, yet it is what we all crave. However, it must be earned or the receiver will never fully appreciate the gift. Seduction is the ultimate form of influence for unconditional love, exemplifying the boldness to pluck a flower from the edge of a precipice.

It is important to remind my reader, here, that we are not talking about fleeting relationships or a ruse to possess, but a genuine desire to embrace your soul mate forever. You must be what you desire needs and be ready to evolve continuously. The art of seduction requires the whispering of love in her ear, the whispering of love in her mouth, the whispering of love in her pearl and the whispering of love in her heart. You must pronounce you care in ways illuminating her soul. You are honoring her feminine flow and nurturing it to grow with sincere communication. Sacred love is dressed in the attributes of physical beauty, mental equilibrium, emotional sensibility, moral purification and spiritual harmony. There is an alluring youthful innocence that is absent of sexual activity, calling to be possessed and will attract the superficial and will intimidate the shy. A person who is dishonest with themselves is incapable of being honest with you and we usually walk into this form of relationship with our eyes wide shut.

CHROMOSOME HORMONE

The idea of someone being born to love you has always intrigued my mind to love more intensely and sincerely. I have always contemplated the balance between genetic compatibility and motivations that drive specific actions in behavior. I have experienced meeting the genetic compatibility in a lover upon the very first glance and I have come to earn a soul through intimate communication or learn a soul through observation in managing challenges. Adversity does have a way of showing who we are at the core, below the surface of the personality we show the world. It is easy to believe what we see every day is real and what we witness in adversity is the intruder. The intruder is our real personality hidden from view. In the same sense, we cannot ignore the truth that steps into the light, as the intruder, when a soul is completely relaxed. A soul possesses no need to guard itself, offering us a glimpse. When you encourage what you witness in these moments, it is a sign of a true connection with the essence of a soul.

There is so much more to explore in this conversation of genes and influenced behavior in the cultivation of love. However, the intent of this prose is to be a guidepost towards encouraging reflection, research and experimentation instead of positioning myself as the solution. We are each unique and our needs evolve as we mature. I remember being blessed, many years ago, with presenting at a Northeastern University forum and advising the students that the real concern from my perspective is not in their adamant belief today, but if in ten to twenty years from now they still believe exactly as they do today. The condition of experience to devalue youthful enthusiasm or for youthful enthusiasm to devalue the patterns learned through experience is a flaw in our thinking about worth. The most amazing and spectacular results emerge when youthfulness and experience dance in harmony.

We are influenced by the experiences of our mother while in the womb and by the messages we consistently experience in our environment as a child, even as we youthfully embrace the challenges of life. When I ponder the narrative of my life it is extremely difficult and actually impossible to precisely isolate generic inheritance from influences in my proclamation of who I am. It is an intelligent sway of identity to advise and alluring to accept my mind is the deity of the universe through the validation of materialist accomplishments. When this message is sincerely extended and reasons successfully with our concerns we will usually embrace the message as truth. Consequently, understanding this balance of materialistic accomplishment and character content requirement for our sense of success and happiness is extremely important in nurturing love.

It is the masculine flow's role to support and encourage the active living of the feminine flow. I understand this reality of expression better than most males and this contributes to the intensely intimate relationships of love I experience with women. I elevate what it means to be feminine, cherishing the quality as precious and the respectful opening. I enter a conversation with a feminine essence and the masculine perspective of how can I support, encourage and contribute to her pure self-actualization. It is my intent to give in an intensely intimate way that adds undeniable value. The opportunity to give in this way is the gift I receive within the relationship. What evolves is our pleasing pleasure expression of what we share. It becomes a depth of conversation that articulates the actuate design of procreation and the role of the 23rd chromosome of the twenty-three pairs of chromosomes. What is true on the biological level is true for our intellectual, emotional, moral and spiritual self too. When we connect the symbolic representations to purpose, understanding is revealed towards nurturing optimum health for life. We must examine our filling fluid composition balance in understanding our perception of acceptable.

Two and three equal five and five represents the circle (zero), spirituality or the unseen. Twenty-three double (pairs) represent sixty-four and doubled One twenty-eight. The circle doubled can represent eight (Byte) or infinity when we rest our case. The intrinsic connection is not by human design, but represented in many ways through human manipulation of the universal design. Within this science of 23rd chromosome there is a specific role in the evolution of life for the X and Y. Two X chromosomes offer life in the formula, that is dependent on the contribution of the Y. It is preposterous to embrace a woman (XX) not needing a man (XY), even as we observe eight (Byte) limbs with the two X chromosomes. I will connect this with a bias of my own a little later. However, what is totally unacceptable in this formula of human life is an YY dual. I am an advocate for human life, preserving your biological inheritance and understand the connection with my preferences. I surmise the distorting of this inheritance is our reach in being a deity and not bound by this biological statement for human life. We introduce the rationalization of the foundational tripartite nature in scripture, known to some as the Trinity, as a virgin excluded from heavenly recognition in the formula. We have twisted the two leg limbs into one, deforming the correct role of woman (womb of mind) in creation.

There are so many ways to look at this biological science and continuously connect the concepts to better understand my message. However, I want to transition with the concept of balance. With two legs at the appropriate angle it is very difficult to push her over to the right or the left. When you inset a third leg, at the appropriate angle, it is extremely difficult to push her over backwards or forward. The singular leg of the male should provide support for balance in representing the tripartite for human life. She must sense the sincerity of your intentions and willingness\ability to please as a soothing chemistry exchange gaining and retaining the connection or her right to life. The flavor of play will rise spontaneously in the moment and enhance the influence of your mutual caring. Understanding the depths of her why forges a bond that transcends the object of act itself.

I remember one such moment clearly during a serious conversation concerning religious practice and religious understanding. In that moment I mention becoming a Hajji even though I never physically made the pilgrimage to Mecca. In a seductive tone her lips cooed genuinely, "Yes! You are my hot G." The playful pun on the sound was delicious and brought a smile to my face. In these moments you realize a deeper love is always absolutely possible. You must wear the garment of sexual elegance intentionally and gracefully, creating the spectrum of passive or active sexual tension you desire within intimate communication. It is the variety in the menu that offers more than a single shot sex signature and more of mastering the multiple stimulation signature in sexual intimacy. The decision of what is best for you and your mate flows through the communication of learning. You must gain an astute understanding of who she was, is and will be. It is an attribute of the maturity in knowing yourself, as you evolve as a living organism and nurtures a sustaining relationship of pleasing pleasure. Too many of the progressive works on sexuality articulated advice is influencing us to disfigure our natural self within this expression of uniqueness. It is not wise to defy the natural order of duality in creation or confuse the principles of our physical reality with mystic perceptions of the divine. Our mind dictates who we can be as a lover beyond the natural prowess we are born with genetically. I can still vividly remember the Brookline sign, "Hire a teenager today, while they still know everything.", offering me a scientific glimpse into selection.

The symbiotic relationship of a cell within a cell that we define as Mitochondria DNA plays a critical role in natural selection, as a genetic history provider and an energy (determinate) enhancer. Mitochondrial DNA is unique in many ways, but I will focus on two (base pairs) here towards making a point for consideration and to guide the flow of my scientific glimpse. As a DNA Mitochondrial is packaged in chromosomes within the nucleus and possesses its own genetic material that is provided by the mother only. The suggestion here is that the female essence is even within the Y chromosome. The observation illuminating my conscious is born through the science of chromosomes. I am specifically referencing the sex X and Y chromosome determining gender provided by the male. The princely posture, the powerful eye contact, the warm smile, the sexy aroma and the resonance voice are a male's feminine grace harmoniously dancing with her passions for masculine dominance. The selection and arrangement of words offer meaning only understood by the intrigued soul. You are chosen even before the first word vibrates her ear and only acts as a confirmation to what is already known.

Listen to the heartbeat of my words and witness the magic of love transforming certainty into possibility within the invisible massage of my therapy. I am intentionally being brief and simultaneously offer you much to consider. A hint to the wise is sufficient! The brevity is intentional in hopes of minimizing confusion and containing disruption to your perception of self as a purposeful medium destination. We can easily identify that the male Y chromosome is missing a limb in comparison to the female X chromosome upon observation. Standing on one leg builds strength and standing on two distributes the weight. When the sufficient strength is developed and balancing mastered we can stand effortlessly on one leg, but walking will continuously remain a challenge in contrast to walking on two legs. I am suggesting that this chromosome deformity is directly connected to a male feeling blessed with a phallus, woman I know proclaim as a third leg. The leg that grows and displays its brilliance through erection within sexual stimulation or the expression of attraction. I believe it is naturally connected to why males, in general, are so insecure about performance and we are focused on tangible results or fixing.

Within the science of numbers when you present two characters or digits you possess four options (the X Chromosome). The two characters represent duality in creation and the four options represent the physical world symbolically. In other words, you have the option of two X chromosome, one X chromosome and one Y chromosome, one Y chromosome and one X chromosome (order of operation or place value influence) or two Y chromosome. However, within the natural selection for human existence there is no place in our biological life for two Y chromosome. The implications of this observation is profound and controversial when measured through sexual relationships. The irony is that just as Mitochondrial is the mother's contribution for both male and female the Y chromosome is the father's contribution for a son. The two X chromosomes offer eight options or the erect symbol of infinity. You hear a lot about the power of the subconscious mind in the media today and the unseen governing the seen for what is possible in our life. With opportunity the power of our subconscious mind does influence what is possible, but opportunity is offered by influences beyond our control and choices claimed before our birth. When blessed, we arrive at a moment where we can decide how to respond and character is fate.

I understand there is no way for me to justly discuss the implications of my thought in this chapter without it becoming a book within itself. However, we must be willing to look on a biological level to recognize social influences morphing our passions. We will make very diverse decisions and I am sure there will be one we will respectfully disagree, but as an educator I often advise my students in making conscious decisions grounded in research and reflection. It is part of my sincerity of intentions philosophy. There is a guidepost in the consideration of the symbol "Y" carrying the sound of the word why, encouraging us to explore purpose. My numerological reference of chromosome pattern is connected to my understanding of the binary byte and the message in a symbol. The principles that support the technological advances we experience is not in any way complete, but form an expression of what is possible. What I sense as true today will evolve as my perception is transformed through experiences and reflection. Two twenty on February 20, 2020 continuously rises through impressions messaging my conscious mind. The succession of zeros and twos (022002202020) is my convergence of science, technology and numerology in defining fate. What will be has already happened in the Omnipresence of Allah. On this date, at this time, you will witness what I sense today, as destiny, clocked into my chromosome at birth. I will not attempt to pre-determine what will actually be revealed, but I would advise you to investigate similar patterns in your life to prevent the squandering of opportunity. I am not celebrating my sixtieth for the commonly traditional reasons, as I point you two years into the future and purge myself in preparation of what will be.

ARTISTIC INFUSION

The value represented in the symbol of a number is a picture worth a thousand words, infusing a message in the art of communication and is intended to massage self-actualization. The art presented in this book is an artistic manifestation of my vision. It is directed towards exemplifying the beauty words alone cannot acknowledge and compliment the words in the same breath. The synopsis of my vision as I presented it to the artist was titled "Love" and how self-love guides how we love others. The cover is a simplistic expression of the more complex images offered at the beginning of the three parts in this book. Realizing the depths of my message flowing through the art I decided the cover needed to be an easy lift, for the reader to take the first step on a journey in love. When in doubt, supply the pressure and she will provide movement. The orgasm will arrive when there is no resistance and the reader is open to hearing my message. It is about you claiming yourself and accepting I desire only what you are willing to offer freely. I truly desire what is best for you and I only want to possess what is rightfully mine.

I did learn a lot about local artist and how they managed the complexity of my request. In my attempt to be earnest and protective of my budget I learned something about myself in the process. It is about becoming better with every breath I take and forging stronger relationships towards a common good. The complexity of the art requested there is the image of two women and one man.

The darkest hue woman represents the source or freedom to love and is represented by the wing of a bird. The man represents the seat of power, protection and prosperity as symbolized in the Choku Rei. Choku Rei as a Reiki Power Symbol or place the power of the universe here. The second woman symbolizes the future or fertility with the palm leaf. Together we are the boundless energy evolving playfully to manifest maturity through the vibrations of the subconscious collective continuous flow designed to preserve the good in what we build. Way too often living the life distracts us from building a life. The art captures and amplifies my unadulterated journey, lined with esoteric wisdom, and evolving into the explicit expression of love.

The vision is intended to just be a framework for an artist's colorful interpretation and expression. I talked to them about each of the images having very distinctive, robust and firm Nubian (African-American) features to represent the exquisite beauty of love supreme. My desire was for the strong features to flow into an abstract creativity and touched with vibrant expression. The darkest hue woman, representing freedom should possess a dominate pose in the art. The diversity in hue complexion is intended to represent completeness. The strong and youthful characteristics should capture the soul of our essence. Abstractly included are the three symbols of freedom, power and fertility embodying purpose. Fertility should be very sensual, sexy and alluring.

THE REAL THING

I love to love intensely and sincerely, purposely being mindful for what is best beyond the initial urge to possess the beauty capturing my attention. I must consistently evaluate and purge my intentions as any relationship evolves to grasp its true purpose in my life. Interest, attraction, laughter and flattery are four primary variations of seduction. Each has its own attribute requiring a specific caress to be visible as love and in reality are vibrations of love. Within the spectrum of frequencies there are vibrations we cannot hear with our physical ear, yet they still influence what is possible for us to hear. In this way seduction can be conscious, unconscious, intentional or unintentional. In some intimate way who I am offers what you need and resting in the fertile soil of your soul. We will respond in contrast to the depths of our frustrations through denied passions in search of compatible anchors. We should never ignore the ways our actions harm the innocent when giving self to denied passions. I am always mindful of the children in determining what is best as my ultimate gift of love.

It is about giving my best and honest communication despite how flawed I am as a "Y" chromosome. We may find justification to deform or distort our natural design, but we cannot change the foundational laws or principles of creation. Truth is not statistical! I will always remember the inscription on the inside cover of my college statistics book stating in bold print "There are lies, dame lies and then statistics." In the movement of Big Data, the intention is to identify your attitude, aptitude, intelligence, intensity and integrity in order to place you within specific tribes for a designed purpose. With enough information the algorithm can precisely predict what I can sell you as fact. The algorithm is accurate based on the assumptions provided and the real influence is to align your perception of self with these assumptions. Ironically, seduction's aim is to explore your attitude, aptitude, intelligence, intensity and integrity in solidifying the relationship. When our intentions are pure we aim to strengthen the weaknesses and when we have ulterior motives we aim to exploit weaknesses. There are those moments when a person is not ready to do what is best and I will exploit the weakness for the greater good of the soul I love.

In my career as an educator I have moved into leadership positions, became a career coach and discovered the necessity of being a life coach. In my experience I have found women to be the most transparent and males to be more guarded. There are always exceptions forming their own pattern in defining self and this is an independent discussion we need to have at another time. In a discussion about love with my optometrist she mentioned the need for a non-perverted book about male to male love. I acknowledge and agree with her reasoning, but realized immediately the complications of such a work. I have spent my life understanding women and handling men, even in the process of raising my children. The way in which I love a male is very different than the way I love a woman, even when romance or sexual expression is nowhere on the radar with a woman. However, I believe there are a few common characteristics of a lasting marriage or intimate relationship. The individual in the relationship with you is either content, distracted, desperate, sacrificial or deceptive.

Taking a moment to understand the why is movement towards exploring the complexities of intent and touches the sincerity of your lover's soul. Discovering you are uncontrollably attracted to the foundational darkness of your lover illuminates a more intense enlightenment of your lover's light. You will become swooned in ways unimaginable without this insight. I am suggesting you will understand yourself better and therefore make better decision for the progression of your life. It will translate into a more authentic relationship when discussed honestly. The ultimate challenge in the process of self-actualization is the continuous growth adjustment, embedded the subconscious justification to avoid tempting the unacceptable. The fear of tasting the unacceptable will encourage us to seek a place of content and abandon being desperate for better.

It is comforting to nurture a relationship that provides what you need, achievable to maintain a relationship while focused on other priorities, unhealthy to stay as a price to pay for some flaw in your character, and an indication of mental illness to remain out of neediness. Too often there is an unspoken arrangement in relationships spanning across decades and that deception is the pulse of expectation. The fulcrum point for each of us is different and should be respected even when you cannot accept it. The chaos in the world is only a reflection of our inner turmoil. Seduction calms the turmoil and can even heal given the opportunity. The true form of seduction is directed towards giving and providing. Marriage should be a merger for better and not a commitment of bondage. Your lover should discover freedom in the relationship and experience pleasures that soothe the soul.

"Khalid, I love you...

I feel a release of pure air(energy) into my heart, in the way you can really understand who and how I feel has me astonished with belief in that you are one whose light illuminates in the darkness. I don't know what to say. .it scares me. Everything I see that seems to be negative about myself you seem to illuminate the positive light in my darkness. I do feel your energy in my yoni. My first encounter wasn't inside of me, but I placed her by my heart so she can feel my rhythm. She spoke to me the moment I put her near. Before I sleep your name is always the last breath I speak before Allahu Akbar. There was a night where I woke from my sleep whispering out your name. Our connection is truly stronger than I could ever imagine between two people, and this is why some people can see change in the way we move almost like we're in sync.

I too want what's best for us, and if we are designed for each other than I want nothing less and I rather have nothing more than to be able to share my moments here in this life with you. Do I see that ever happening? Only Allah knows! Our paths have crossed and aligned as one for the moment and it feels divine as we feel our way with each other, but the reality is we will never know how long it will last. You enjoy and see life with an open mind and have a great outlook on the unseen, where I have much hesitation and I have conditioned myself to be very skeptical as to what paths I should choose. I have chosen quite a few difficult paths, and to be honest have failed immensely at some that have left scars and just won't heal properly. You encourage me to be who I was designed to be, and I thank you for having belief and seeing the light beneath my thick walls.

It took me two days to write my thoughts for you. I'm not the best at expressing myself, I just never felt my words were understood till now, and just laid upon deaf ears. That's all for now... Khalid! You're my most intimate friend and I don't want to lose you, I need you, your passion, your sensitivity, your darkness, your love teaches me to see the light that illuminates from within. Truth, I'm afraid..."

FEMININE FELIDAE

As the lyrics of L'amour Toujours stream from your lips I remember the moisture of their sweetness on mine. You are forever my feminine felidae, never absent from my mind, with an essence that is mine. There is a taste of you that can never be possessed by another and has remained unclaimed by the marriage bond or the healthy family life you have designed. I honor your sacred union, respect your submission to guard, in obeying the command of Allah. Within all beauty I see you and seeing you I witness the beauty in all. The feelings we share are a glimpse of Paradise that is thine. I hear my name in every breath you chime. Our love reaches beyond the eon of time, touching your soul divine, never defined by truths that confine. Cacao Snow Crystal of mine, offering an illuminating glow of joy, shining from inside. I hear your plea, urging me to embrace your sensual view, as I slide within the grasp of your passion. Unconditional is a condition! I will remember! I will anticipate! I will remember.

I truly enjoyed sharing a first with you!

Khalid I love you...

I feel a release of pure air(energy) into my heart, the way you can really understand who and how I feel has me astonished with belief in you that you are one whose light illuminates in the darkness. I don't know what to say, but that it scares me everything I see that seems to be negative about myself you seem to illuminate the positive light in the darkness. I do feel your energy in my yoni. My first encounter wasn't inside of me, but I placed her by my heart, so she can feel my rhythm. She spoke to me the moment I put her near. Before I sleep your name is always the last, just before Allahu Akbar, breath I speak. There was a night where I woke from my sleep whispering out your name. The connection is truly stronger than I could ever imagine between two people and this is why some people can see change in the way we move almost like we're in sync.

I too want what's best for us, and if we are designed for each other than I want nothing less and I rather have nothing more than to be able to share my moments here in this life with you. Do I see that ever happening? Only Allah (SWT) knows. Our paths have crossed and aligned as one for the moment and it feels divine as we feel our way with each other. But, the reality is we will never know how long it will last. You enjoy and see life with an open mind and have a great outlook on the unseen, where I have much hesitation and I have conditioned myself to be very skeptical as to what paths I should choose. I have chosen quite a few difficult paths and to be honest have failed immensely at some that have left scars and just won't heal properly. You encourage me to be who I was designed to be, and thank you for having belief and seeing the light beneath my thick walls.

It took me two days to write to you my thoughts, for you. I'm not the best at expressing myself, I just never felt my words were understood till now, and just laid upon deaf ears. that's all for now. Khalid you're my most intimate friend and I don't want to lose you, I need you, your passion, your sensitivity, your darkness, your love teaches me to see to see the light that illuminates from within. Truth I'm afraid...

Here is the love story you requested, my Feminine Felidae. I believe you will enjoy it, especially knowing I delivered upon request for your pleasure. Please sit down and relax before you begin the read.

Once upon a time...

In the lowest valley of Africa was born a girl by the great nomad Nubian ruler, who travelled the continent claiming every beautiful woman his right to possess. Her mother, the Queen of the valley, was left to raise her daughter and forbidden by law to marry. In his native tongue, not understood by the people of the valley, he named his daughter Yoni and proclaimed one day her charms will be known throughout every palace of Africa. The years past and Yoni matured into the most radiant woman ever. It became necessary to build a special place for her reside and was instructed to never be seen or others will demand to possess her as her mother was possessed by the Nubian ruler. It was anticipated Yoni would die from thirst and starvation in her secluded residence under the roots of the biggest tree in the valley. When her mother returned to declare her dead, six months later, in amazement the secluded borrow was illuminated with virility and smelled of sweet nectar. Yoni informed her mother of the man she envisioned in her dreams and proclaimed her destiny to wed him. Of course, she knew nothing about him and did not even know his name.

On the highest mountain in Africa was born a boy from peasant slaves. He was dropped from his mother's womb onto infested dead meat, as she continued to work. At the end of the work day she took the boy home and handed him to her oldest daughter to care for. Without a name it was suggested by a visitor to call him Lingam and the boy responded with a smile. He grew into a teenager and was put to manual labor of slaughtering wild boars. When he slept his dreams were illuminated with a light and soon a voice from within the light starting asking him his name. During his long days of work and would imagine living the mountain and finding the voice of his dreams. It was his determination to be the Aziz of the kingdom that ruled his people. Lingam plotted and planned his great escape into a life of ease. His parents did everything to discourage him and advise him to let go of such foolish ideas of voices within light and becoming the Aziz of Mali. One evening, on the sunset of his eighteenth birthday, he called back to the voice in his dream "I am the Aziz of Mali." Yoni sprang awoke dripping wet as thick cream flowed from between her firm, dark thighs.

Her mother, the Queen of the Valley, was very concerns and started to prepare her daughter for marriage. If the elders decided Yoni had lost her virginity before marriage, under the supervision of her parents, the whole family would be put to death as the custom of purity required. Yoni proclaimed she would only marry the Aziz of Mali. When the Aziz of Mali heard of the exquisite beauty of Yoni and the vibrancy of her virility he agreed without hesitation. It was all arranged and great wealth was promised the Queen of the Valley. When finally arrived, after travelling across the continent, stepping out of the grand coach Yoni realized it was not the face in her dream. Yoni believed that this man she was marrying was actually the royal representative of the Aziz and when she returned to his home she would find the real Aziz waiting for her. The ceremony was amazing and the Aziz left great wealth as promised. Yoni was absolutely convinced of her belief when the Aziz did not consummate the marriage that evening and they were off to the Kingdom of Mali at the first streak of dawn. The days came and left without the Aziz ever attempting to consummate the marriage. Once they arrived he put Yoni up and elegant wing of the palace with only female servants. Yoni was elated in anticipation of meeting her real husband, who captivated her completely.

Lingam ran free at the crack of dawn one morning, heading to his destiny to be the Aziz of Mali and meet his exquisite wife. He experienced many trials and challenges on his long journey. Killing whatever, man or animal, that stood in his path of destiny. He took their belongings and posed as the person he killed. He finally joined an army heading to Mali to conquer the corrupt kingdom. The general of the army dress in all black, vowing to never show his face until the kingdom was defeated. When the army confronted the Mali kingdom in battle the was lasted for months. They were losing the battle and the general was contemplating retreat. Determined to win the battle and become the Aziz of Mali Lingam killed the general and took his identity. On the secluded wing within the castle the Aziz had started sending one to three men a night has sex with Yoni. Men would come from all over, paying huge sums of wealth for one evening of the illuminating haven of sexual pleasure. Each night Yoni convinced herself this was the rituals of the kingdom, because the real Aziz of Mali did not want a virgin or inexperienced lover. To her surprise she loved sex and the more sex she had the more abundant her nectar flowed. It went from one to three, to three to five and five to nine men an evening before the kingdom was finally overthrown by the Black Armor General.

All the males of Mali were killed and the woman brought forth for distribution as booty. Yoni's beauty and sexual vibrancy was obvious. The Black

Armor general approached her and slowly took off his helmet. By the art of war, he was officially the Aziz of Mali. When Yoni glanced into his face she burst out in excitement, "My Aziz of Mali" and rushed towards him. When Lingam heard the voice he knew immediately it was the voice that had forged this day. As they embraced and kissed passionately for the very first time the army realized the Lingam was the youth who joined them and could not be their true Black Armor General. Five swords were drawn and pieced through both of them, as they gazed into each other's eyes. The brilliant light of Yoni's illuminating haven enveloped them, swooning every soul into submission. Love Supreme Eternalized!

PEARLS OF WISDOM

I was tempted to title this chapter "Boo Koo" due to the complexity, multiple meanings and the typical absence of this message when discussing seduction. It sells to discuss the sweet flavor of seduction and the many benefits when executed correctly. However, to execute seduction correctly, difficulty plays a critical role in the process. It is the tension and pain in forging the relationship that is the true solidifying ingredient for a lasting relationship. It is the intensity of pain that validates the love you feel is real and defies intellectual reasoning. The pain actually draws you closer and a love you never knew existed within rises to the surface.

Harmony is the Boo (girlfriend) Koo (primary aim is to gain, retain and sustain) love full of tears over the years. The only way to explain is to let you hear the message through our communication, as a means of awakening your mind. We entered the room from different doors, where there is no escape, so here we are struggling to understand. I open with a poem written to me by Harmony.

Tell me !
In words
What your eyes have already shown
me
I need to hear it.

I long to feel it.
I want to touch it.
I yearn to taste it.
"Your Love"

Just wanted to let you know that you have been on my mind "all day long" (obviously all night too). You are so embedded in my thoughts that you seem to be all I think about all the time. I feel joy and sadness at the same time. Two emotions that are opposite one another, creating confusion in my mind and in my heart. I keep asking myself what should I do and the answer keeps coming up "you". You will not allow me to be with you and yet I cannot bear the thought of choosing to be without you. What have I gotten my heart into? Is it just me or do you feel the same way? Will I be forced to settle for whatever you say it can be, because you are committed to someone else or should we decide to let go. I only complicate things for you and for that I am sorry. Life and Love are not always fair are they? Somehow I always manage not to get what I really want or need. This I am used to. What

I am not used to is the degree of hurt that comes with it. No, I am not feeling down on myself nor do I feel unworthy, it just is what it is. I am not even sure you feel the same depth of feelings for me as I do for you. For whatever reason you do not always speak what you feel, you simply choose to agree with my sentiments when I speak on them. We did agree on being honest, open and real. Just once, would you allow yourself to be free with me??? Can you trust me enough to give me that?

It is me again. I will try to make this the last email for a while. I am sure you have had enough of me by now. I tossed and turned all night because I was thinking about you and the situation that is before us. I am beginning to believe that this whole thing with you and I is all a test. Why else would we be put back at the table? The first time love was blind and not expressed, everything was wide open except our eyes. Well, actually I knew how I felt. This time we are fully aware of what is on the table and mutual feelings have been expressed. Why have we been brought back to this?

I ask this because the timing for you is a spiritual one, Ramadhan, "a process used for putting yourself in check to continue your forward motion and re-evaluation of your actions and intent." The outcome of the decision is now based on mutual sentiments shared by both of us. It is with great difficulty you must make a decision. Khalid, I am very sorry I have created such a dilemma for you by expressing what is in my heart. Please believe me when I say that it is just as painful for me.

The circumstances have obviously changed in your life but, we stand with love in our hearts and the knowledge of it. You bring to the table love and fear and I bring only love. You bring fear because of what it at stake for you to lose if you choose to love me, so therefore your decision not to love me will be controlled by your fear. I see you stand as faithful, loyal, respected, respectful, and strong to what you have but, yet confused about what could be. If you choose to love me I see you stand as faithful, loyal, respected, respectful and strong to your heart and what could be but yet again confused because fear will also control your decision. It is with great difficulty I am sure that you have allowed yourself to take this all on. No matter what is decided you come out on top because either way there will be someone there for you fulfilling your life in some way. There will also be pain for someone to bear no matter what it decided, this is the downside of life decisions.

From where I stand there is a greater chance that I will lose but, the only fear I have is of losing you and my fear it is not at the table. Sad to say but, I am used losing. Either way I will always love you, nothing could ever change that fact. I have never loved this way before and even though the outcome may not be what I would like it to be I can't give up the way I feel; it just is not an option for me. You chose to be where you are because that is what you want or need. If the impression, I made on your mind and heart then was such that even today I am in your thoughts constantly (at least this is what you tell me) then you would have chosen to seek me out. So, not necessarily being the

best outcome of the situation still leaves a
situation. I am still here and still loving you.

How is it that we have been brought back to one
another again after all the time that has passed
and the changes that have taken place in our lives?
Why are we here? I know that even during your
absence I never stopped loving you. I am confused
only by the reason we are here; a reason I do not
even know. Do you? We will always be as we have
been, being special to one another in some way.
There is always "the place where our shared energy
resides." A place that can never be dissolved. I
know that this is not all about me so do not think
for a minute that I have overlooked this fact. I am
only expressing myself.

Hopefully, at some point we can put all this to rest
and move on.

I have mentioned, in this script, how the seducer must first be seduced and yet it was love at first sight for Harmony. The seduction of my presence arrived long before my physical presence and fate cannot be denied. When I pleaded for Harmony to share the communications, she preserved over the years, I never anticipated the realization of how I neglected to properly respond to her pain. I often mentioned how I did not want to hurt her, but my actions intensified the pain and deepened the love. It is a cruel joke, in an ironic kind of way, how such a pure love can be this way. I have always been honest with Harmony, even though I was blind in very specific ways until today. As I place these words to print, for the very first time, I have decided to define what is on my mind. I will honor our love, in a way, never anticipated in the design, to align our words with time.

"Saxophone sounds playing melodies in my mind. Music of my life vibrating on the notes of my experiences from whence I come. The instrument croons softly of who I am, by telling you my story while leaving impressions on your mind."

I can always visualize the most erotic outcomes to my plans and have learned to brace myself for the most ironic, learning through the convergence of my thoughts and actions. It is here where the absolute reality appears, converging ideas together to form a completely unexpected innovative third solution. The most innovative explorations manifest within the crescendo and is forged through the pain recognize in the birth of life. It is also the fuel of passion that energizes us with the intensity to change, or the contemplation embedded in a pleasure deferred.

Harmony, I love you, in a way I have loved no other and what that means is not what you need, but I am what will be. One Forty-Three from me to thee, over a dinner prepared by me for thee. Success, will be defined, tonight by how we express the unspoken. Between the bites and sips of cuisine, you will hear the most personal details, in a very relaxing and jovial flow of words. The trust we possess will be tested through the substance of purity. The scrumptious meal will moisten our palate, as the privacy of my abode provides the ambiance. A foreplay combination to indulge candidly in a moment long overdue. The tour comes to a locked door and you notice the panties basket near the threshold, what will you do in understanding the rules.

A new day has dawned. The Sun is not out to warm our faces, as we pass through the space of time. Today, the sun only shines as we pass through the state of our minds. As we shine a new day has dawned. Peace and Harmony.

I am blessed to have you in my life and I will never take what you offer me for granted, nor will I betray your trust. You are the breath of balance in every love, cultivating our urge to be complete and give completely.

AMOROUS SEDUCTION

Bloom walked into the room with an impetuous confidence, motivated through a visceral sensation to hear my voice once more before the evening drifts away. Our eyes meet, as I gaze in her direction, to observe the excitement dancing in her mind. Bloom's labium becomes firm as Oxytocin is released and moister forms between her thighs. She pauses to savor the yearning in her palate and to decide on an artful approach. Slowly, my gaze glides down her neck to rest on a pair of the most succulent breast a man could ever imagine tasting. I could visibly see Bloom's nipples harden beneath the fabric as we communicated without an audible word.

Within the moment I focused on the challenge she was contemplating in her mind. I reflected on the treat of such exquisite beauty seeking to seduce and marveled the courage in her approach. I turned to Vanilla, whispering expressions of my uninhibited passion, in anticipation of what was about to happen. It was my intention to greet seduction with seduction, forming an amorous circle of expression. Vanilla has always been an adventurous soul willing to please for the pleasure of the experience and it excited her to comply with my request. Influence must always be wielded appropriately, as a sign of respect for the gift.

Bloom approaches us with a cordial greeting and a tantalizing question that only I could answer. Instantly I knew she would be my creamy toy tonight and Vanilla would need very little enticement to enjoy a taste of Bloom's pleasure. She did not earn her affectionate title of "Vanilla Pleasance" as an innocent observer, even though she is usually inclined to deny. Vanilla loves being the women who lures other woman, signaling her desire to taste both.

I move closer towards Vanilla, as I direct my attention to Bloom, brushing my bicep across her left nipple and resting my hand on the inner muscle of her thigh. She quivers beneath my touch and smiles with appreciation as I answer the question with deliberate care. My answer canopied a question intended for both Vanilla and Bloom, as to isolate everyone else, in the room, from the conversation. In this moment is where most people excuse themselves or listen in for a lesson or two. The warmth in the ambiance, of the room, increases noticeably and it is my turn to dance. Standing before us is a vibrantly tender lady encouraging the touch of my magic wand. I am seduced as I move to seduce.

The question asked, by Bloom, is "when two people find each other what should keep them from being together?" Her gaze only left my eyes momentarily to include Vanilla and isolate everyone else. The aura of unrestraint vive of desire was in the air and I paused to enjoy the aroma. I confidently answer, as Vanilla whispers, "Nothing!", keeping my gaze. The conversation slowly glides into fantasies and circumstances inhibiting us from what is best for the heart. The content of the conversation became more intimate, so we stepped out onto the balcony for a whiff of cool night air and a little more privacy. The bright moon light and stars lit the sky perfectly with a mysterious and sensual accent of romance to our dance of seduction. We may not realize it, but one of the primary purposes in seduction is to build trust and romance solidifies that mutual trust.

The formula of trust that builds the healthiest relationships is laced with sincerity and purity of intentions. It does not dish up a dark pain, but a pain illuminating light with the best intentions. The jovial disposition of the Frolic can often be misunderstood as immaturity and the deeper intent of good is missed. The distinctive difference is uncovered through the evidence of deep thought given to the conversation. It is a dance of seduction only appreciated by the blessed few, respecting love as a precious gift.

Figure 3 Percy Davis - Artist

PART TWO –

ROMANCE

I love you! Not only for who you are. But for who I am when I am with you.

I love you! Not only for who you are making yourself. But for who you are making me.

I love you! For the part of me that you bring out.

I love you! For putting your hand into my heaped-up heart.

And loving all the foolish, weak things that you can't help dimly seeing there.

Drawing out into the light all the beautiful belongings that no one else had looked quite far enough to find.

I love you! Because you are helping me to make of the lumber of my life.

Not a tavern, but a temple out of works of my every day.

Not a reproach, but a song.

I love you! Because you are doing more, than any creed could do, to make me good and more than any fate could do to make me happy.

You have done it! Without a touch. Without a word. Without a sign.

You have done it by being yourself and this is the greatest gift of all.

SOUL BALM

Romance is the moments we share in affectionate explorations of love, purposely selected to strengthen the bond for passion. You will hear the voices of pleasing pleasure nurtured for more than ten years that has preserved freshness through explicit expression. The soul balm orated here is about sharing and the lure within its anticipation, offering a picturesque charm to a soul truly appreciating its value. Trust built on a pattern of intimacy designed to establish, beyond the act itself, a nurturing bond of "pleasure pleasing, pleasing pleasure" passion. The art of pleasing pleasure devoted to pleasure pleasing within the purity of love. It is not about putting your best appearance forward, as we tend do when dating, before settling into who we really are. It is about presenting you at the core of your conscience, in the most pristine ways possible, at the point of initial contact. You will be blessed with the poetic voice exemplifying the harmonious taste of seduction and romance, leading to some of the most authentic expressions of passion laced with esoteric wisdom. You will hear a soul offering her heart to a mind earning such trust.

I grew up hearing the phase "the darker the berry the sweater the juice, forming my preference of beauty and appreciation for sisters. There is a very special delight in observing a chocolate sister embracing her complexion as a symbol of royalty and caring for herself meticulously as a reflection of who she is inwardly. Inward expression is much more about how you wear ornaments than what ornament is worn. The interest, activities and opinions we embrace influence our values, attitude and behavior as attributes of character. These attributes are core ingredients towards a soul's happiness, success and sense of freedom. We should strive for material success and prosperity, because it allows us to enjoy a certain quality of life only economic solvency can award. However, materialistic accumulation can be a distraction, causing you to neglect a purpose beyond self-gratification. I am still unsure why my purpose compels me to compose a dance with intense spiritual\moral insights and explicit sexual explorations to emphasize the requirement of balance towards the purity illuminated through sincerity of intentions. I am a firm believer in that our purity within our sincerity of intentions is the key to Paradise.

What we experience here is a sign for what awaits us in the Hereafter, where an extreme hardship can be a punishment or a purging, depending on how we handle the challenge. In the same truth, of duality, materialistic success can be a punishment or purging. The insight of the compounding binary to eight and now one hundred twenty-eight, is a sign offering us vision into infinity. I am reminded of a moment with Berry that clarifies my message in a very special way. It is important to understand that Berry does not like to dominate, lead or repeat herself when it comes to expressing herself romantically. The expectation is for her man to listen, provide and guide as she nurtures, preserves and observes. The shyness is genuine and passionately explosive when caressed correctly. I cannot emphasize enough how amazing love is when your partner is offering what she loves and you love it.

I surprised Berry with a stage performance orated in a language neither of us spoke. As we were walking, after the performance, discussing the message we took away from the performance, the sign emerged. Berry suddenly stopped and gazed into my eyes before offering me a long passionate kiss. The chill of the cold winter night vanished and I started to perspire as warmth consumed my heart. This is her way were words are not necessary to define or explain the moment. There is absolutely a charm in a woman offering what pleases you because she understands it pleases you. However, it is a completely different aphrodisiac and magical medicine to receive what a lover loves and you love it. There are moments where she is enjoying so intensely and I am enjoying it so intensely that I become self-conscious in the fact that the moment is even possible. It is difficult to reconcile intellectually the exquisiteness of giving and receiving becoming one for both simultaneously in sublime delight.

The sign of sublime delight is very similar when seduction and romance occupy the same space at the same time. It is purely magical to offer or embrace an expression of love that is both seductive and romantic in the same breath. The pleasure in the same way the identical expression of love can be seductive in one moment and romantic in another is an infinite sign. Personally, I really enjoy offering a seductive moment of pleasure for a lover that drips with romance in harmony. Witnessing the energy exchange of a seductive moment evolving romantically is a humbling experience in the dance. I often reflect on the seduction that happened at a crowded party and moments later we were walking the shore barefoot discussing our sense of self in the world, just before entertaining ourselves passionately sweating profusely on the dance floor. The experience is seamless, all in a gaze, words would take too long to define and an embrace with a special touch defining volumes. I understand the ease in believing we are primarily discussing sexual relationships, especially after hearing the seductive breath of Berry and the combined delight in part three of this prose. However, I must counsel you here that at least seventy-five percent of my intimate relationships never even hint to sexual explorations. Arousal can be spiritual, moral, emotional, intellectual, physical or a combination of any or all of the mentioned. In this spirit, arousal is always present in every connection of two souls. The Frolic's nature is to amplify the charm towards inhaling her rising from the moisture between her thighs and then allow the moment to calm as a demonstration of kind. I have discovered demonstrating is much more impressive and profound as your declaration of sincerity. Love is a continuous exploration of passion and realization of what is possible. Allow me to be yours...

Within the short duration of our professional relationship Serenity's character appealed to me. In one meeting with her I received the subconscious message of feminine glow I define as the signal to proceed. On the surface she did not do or state anything different, yet the message was clear as we worked out solutions as a group. I am telling you with absoluteness I knew and was willing to examine my sense. When our collective work was complete and everyone was leaving the room I paused Serenity with a question. Once the professional business was handled properly I informed Serenity that I needed to shift our conversation to a more personal tone. When her eyes said yes and lips parted lightly I continued. As I gazed into her eyes I expressed how I desired to know her more intimately. For a moment, I could see the shock on her face that faded into concern. I am sure the usual conversations she receives from men, because of that plump firm round ass, caused her to step back slightly. I smiled at how the depth of my honesty touched her and the concern I was hitting for sex flashed on her face. When she asked me to clarify my intentions I knew then as I know today what is possible. Here we stood in our very first personal communication sharing an exploration for intimacy. It is my intent to romance her with experiences of intimacy no man has considered her worthy of before my arrival.

I usually just arrive unannounced with a clear option for her to decline. She did decline once and we spent three hours talking in the warm summer air. It is critical to display feminine and masculine qualities of seduction in the dance of love. I focus on eliminating any hint of pretense in order to infuse romance into the seduction. The courage to reach for better in linked to how we truly view self and I am committed to better even within casual relationships. The seduction that provides a taste romance and is absent of passionate love making is my specialty. I love loving intimately and preserving passionate lovemaking for honoring love supreme. I know firsthand how lovemaking changes the paradigm of a relationship and am particularly careful in assessing our souls are equally yoked in the process. I live a very complex and complicated life canopying the core of who I am without regret. It is easy to believe you are ready, until you step into my world, to discover realities unimaginable, of intense darkness purging into sublime light.

Romantic explorations are more than the physical objects of beauty in the experience, even though we know the physical ambiance is very influential in solidifying bonds. Imagery evokes emotions and emotions motivate us in so many complex ways. I visited a Which Wich Sandwich Shop and ordered an Avocado Sub with extra meat and extra Avocado. The preparer was ready to process the order when she noticed I had double meat checked off. When she looked up in an awkward attempt explaining there is no meet on an Avocado sub, without insulting my intelligence, I offered her a delightful smile and joyous laugh. I connected with her in a way no one has ever taken the time to do, when making an order. A few minutes later she even came over to our table to express how the experience made her day, cleaned our table and stated that if there was anything I needed to let her know. I thanked her profusely for being such a warm hearted soul and appreciating my demonstration of love. You learn so much about the person in these unadulterated moments and it influences those witnessing the exchange too. I do this often, like walking up to the information desk and asking them if they can direct me to the information desk.

I have discovered an aroma, that I wear often, that is extremely seductive. There is an antique store I often visit to discover unique items for gifts and decoration. As I browsed the five floors of antiques, in my quest for beauty, women ignored the antiques and followed the aroma. I glanced up to see one smiling at me and over my shoulder another with a similar expression. The first commented and the other joined the conversation. We talked about the seductive influence of aroma, my unnamed scent and our attraction to unique beauty. In this moment the aroma was seductive and romantic, because of the uniqueness of the ambiance. The magnetic charge of the two excites passion and we can either honor the moment or guide it into an agenda to serve a thirst. I love making love and Berry knows this better than any woman I have ever been intimate with. You will observe how she massages our passion through sexual explorations in a very romantic way to seduce me when I am miles away. Berry understands how to provide gratification to the degree that I will proclaim her has an adoring aromatic soothing restorative and healing of my soul.

In the words of my Berry I offer you passion, romance and seduction. *"You are on my mind so heavy this morning, and my body yearns for you - to please you, to explore you, to taste you, to feel every inch of you. I cannot have you in the moment, so I wish to spend the day fantasizing about making love to you. The images of our caramel - milk chocolate bodies intertwined dance through my mind.*

I would LOVE to wake you with my lips wrapped around that delicious third leg. I'm not sure if that is me servicing your needs or me servicing my own. You are my king, and it is always my pleasure to serve and honor you. To begin, I want to run my lips along the shaft of your third leg, just enough so that he will stand at attention, begging for more. I want to slide my lips around the crown of my king's lingam savoring the feel of your scepter's head before sliding you deep into my mouth over and over again, covering you fully in wet warmth - the promise of what is to cum.

As my need to have you peaks, I will be overcome with my own desire for you. I will worry that I have lost my focus on pleasing you. Still, I will ask for your permission to ride. If you grant me permission, it will be because you understand that serving me in this way allows me to truly serve you, and I will lower myself onto you, engulfing you in the warmth and wetness you have been waiting for, and then, baby, I will ride....

When I am ready to cum, I will want to be dominated by you, to be reminded that your reign over me is unparalleled. I will want you inside me and your hands all over me. If I can bear the momentary change in position, I will ask that you flip me over, slide that delicious third leg inside me and allow your hand to find its way around my body to my clit. My body will be on fire and I will whisper your name, pleading for you to make me cum. My body will contract and relax with the pleasure of an orgasm that only you can deliver, sending me off into another world of indescribable delight. I will float back down to Earth, turning my attention fully to you.

Your third leg, even after all of that work, will still be erect, wet with our juices, and I will make it my mission to lick and suck every inch of you until you give me the ultimate pleasure of feeling your cum drip down my throat as you find your release. Even at that moment, after I have reminded you that you are my one and only king, and I am the same for you...your queen, I will want more of you. My body will still be craving to experience another climax with you. But the joy of laying by your side will be too much to let go of, and we will lay with each other, sticky in the juices of a love manifested. This, Love, is what I want to do to you, and what I want you to do to me. Enjoy your day, love. Think of me, and smile knowing that you have my love always."

PERSONALITY
TEMPERAMENT

I am Khalid A. Mustafa, here by the command of Allah, as a servant of the Originator of Creation, to illuminate love, on my path to Paradise. The opening sentence answers to the five critical questions every person should be able to state about self. On my journey I discovered the soothing temperament of love to be absolutely breathtaking, intelligent, vibrant and a sexy lady. I am blessed to have you, in so many exquisite ways, as mine. The core charm of my personality is the cultivation of your actualization, blossoming brilliantly, with royalty flourishing within. You are so amazing! It is impossible for you to really comprehend what it is like to love and be loved by you. The vibrations of your temperament resonate harmoniously with mine as the aroma of your dew embraces me as I approach for our first introduction. The eerie sense of knowing someone intimately who you have never met before surprises me. I glance into your eyes and they smile with acknowledgement. It must be my imagination, so I dismiss the idea and focus on a distraction to mask destiny. I was wholly seduced and I could not control the vibration from sentiments flowing through my soul. When I stepped closer to greet you, the sense of our connection is much stronger and your eyes pleaded with me to hear your heart. There is a mountain of practical reasons why our intimate connection was forbidden, yet I moved in to seduce and our moment swiftly evolved into today.

It is very uncomfortable to know we have only touched the surface and are in so deep at the same time. My every nerve fiber yearns to emerge in you. It is a very powerful sensation and I lose my breath just at the thought of it all. As we walk the ocean shore or I watch you dance in the snow, I reflect on the gift of your willingness to love and be loved. The trust we forged opened the door to experiences awarded to no other. Our souls are intertwined and this is what we have always desired. The meaning of "Love" is just not enough to reveal the breadth of emotions swimming through our veins. We acknowledge in an embrace that the ultimate purpose for lovers is freedom. When we are compelled to restrain or contain the purity of our soul, in a marriage, it is a crippling emotional bondage that suppresses or oppresses the full potential of the bond. When we decide to ignore the obvious, the silence stagnates love and shifts the paradigm of growing together. In the twinkle of an eye we commence growing apart and embrace obligation as a form to maintain the relationship. The intended function or purpose of marriage transforms where illness is expected and even encouraged. We dismiss how critical open and honest communication is to the health of a sacred partnership. It is my prayer we continuously remain transparent and willing to confront challenges for better.

The appetite to seduce your lover must remain active and the desire to romance always available in a truly healthy love. The real joy is the selflessness in striving to always work towards what is best for your lover and trust what is best will be yours in the process. It is the unconditional love that carries the condition of happiness and willingness to please. I package this enlighten elevation of love with success in this life and bliss in the Hereafter. We can do good and be successful at the same time. The oxymoron of my paradox is in taming forbidden pleasures through conscience expressions of sincerity within moral self-actualization. I find it impractical to shun the inclinations of pleasures influenced by stimulations seducing me wherever I turn my head. The experiences and circumstances that form me will guide me to who I must be to serve properly. It is common for us to commit to the institution of religion or the politics of faith and neglect the fundamental value of religion as sincerity. Our faith must be more than belief, as it explores the boundaries of trust. I have learned to embrace my faults and sins with the intent to purge and live authentically as a flawed mind requiring Allah's Mercy, Forgiveness and Salvation to achieve

Paradise. My faith in the victory of good compels me to trust that my plea to Allah will purify my heart and soul far beyond any other action I can take.

There will be text in this script causing you to pause and even doubt the spiritual\moral guidance in my message. We live in the existence of duality, no matter how deeply we walk into the light, mandating a balance with darkness. I have decided to confront, enlighten and reveal my darkness in prayer that I can assist the multitude of misguided victims of broken relationships. Please accept my words, as a guidepost towards healthy relationships, as a cure for the many ills we witness perpetrated through selfish pursuits. Whereas others may consider the physical world as reality I see it as an expression of the unseen reality governing the laws of the seen. The physical attraction of a woman gets my attention, but does not retain my attention. It is extremely important to take notice of how a woman cares for herself, in the way she dresses and compliments her core sense of self. It is more about the content of character supporting the appearance that is the most seductive in my eye. The pleasures we embrace in this life should be a taste of the fruit in the Hereafter. In the framework of duality, we have good and bad, but with the oneness of Allah it is all good. The pleasure of pleasing within pleasing pleasure is the absolute best of what life blesses us with. The Alpha and Omega of success is the praise of the Originator of Creation in all things.

Possessing the reign of influence over a wonderful, sexy and amazing woman is truly frightening and an exhilarating blessing in the same breath. The bad boy is exhilarated by the possibilities and the good man is frightened by understanding the seriousness of accountability in abusing such an influence. A real mind embraces the pleasures and astutely honors the moral purity of the gift. I desire to explore the deepest recesses of your soul in my reign, in my quest to delight you with pleasing pleasure never imagined possible. Unfortunately, or should I declare fortunate for me that most males are conditioned to be takers. We are condition to take and possess, leaving their partner unsatisfied in the journey. The imbalance warps our perception of pleasure and unnatural desires for pain emerge as a cure. I bear witness to the heights of darkness and depths of light one mind can perspicacious acknowledge in the pursuit of wisdom.

The sagacious art of love is to give more than is required and be more than ever anticipated. You can always be present despite any distance of time. Truth is not in the act alone, but the pattern of illuminating the soul and delighting the heart. The sparks forming forever mutual attraction is incomprehensible and harmonizes beneath all of our conscious efforts in seduction. The embedded duality in this observation encompasses our humanity as compatible opposites comprising our fabric of harmony. The fundamental ingredient in marketing to influence perception is repetition and that is equivalent to character in relationships. The pattern of character will emerge with repetition, through seven intense distinctly diverse experiences with a person. The symbolic application of the number seven offers us a glimpse into the foundation of who a person really is despite what they articulated. Seven is the sign of completeness and perfection, symbolizing what you will always be and revealing your heart of hearts. Always, in all ways!

The instinctive impulse we default to when the unexpected crashes into our life defines who we are in a way no other observation can provide. It continues to surprise me how the unexpected influences the flow of my words when trying to capture a thought. I intend to dot a reminder and look up three paragraphs later with a completely different message. The trust in feeling I can write what is on my heart offers a freedom of expression in the never ending story in creating this guide. We will discuss so many intimate and taboo thoughts on our heart and soul in our willingness to understand. Who would imagine or even believe we are so compatible, until they witness us sharing the love illuminating from our pleasing pleasure. I am breathlessly in awe at the possibilities in the balm in our palm. I do not take your precious gift for granted and constantly ponder how to continuously earn your love. My prayer is that our intimacy grows despite circumstances and that we will always embrace the good discovered in the other. I love you more than words can ever express and I realize that all paths in my life guided me to you. I am forever a digit text away from your warm embrace and encourage your courage to trust the connection, that will never be abused or taken for granted. Thank you so much for the delight I have never known and will always illuminate my soul with joy and happiness. With the last breath of each day I proclaim we must never despair the soothing Mercy of Allah and what sincerity of intentions can cultivate.

The joy of our explorations and mutual self-actualization should reign supreme over the challenges embedded in this fleeting life. It is here where we rejoice in the delights of physical expression evolving into spiritual actualization. The mystic essence of reality is pure and divine, elevated high above the worldly passions of sexual expression. The pursuit is to suffuse your spirit with the love, memories and passions reserved for my arrival, to claim the endowment for your soul. When your spirit recognizes my value, happiness will forever be with you. I urge you to feel the joyfulness in really knowing me and fearlessly deepen the intimate connection of our souls. There will be times when distance denies me your touch and still I will be blessed with a reminder of the beauty in your touch. The flower smiling at me from between the high blades of grass to the magnificent artwork radiantly displaying to attract me, I pause to reflect on the beauty of you.

Wisdom suggests that if you want reality unmasked the beauty in learning the difference between destructive activities and becoming the change agent from good to great, you must be willing to experience death. We must die in this life to enter our home of Paradise and we must die to one conscience of perception as we are born into the illumination of another. The paradox is that what we often perceive as destruction precedes renewal and what we think is the greatest blessing is the most destructive. It is in the formula of good getting in the way of great, or in the consciousness of distance nurturing growth. I embrace the darkness in order to see correctly in the light. Those who shun the difficulty of facing the enlightenment of darkness will never explore the extraordinary glory resting in the seed. I advise you to look at the sacrifice made for every great accomplishment and you will see the folly in clinging to the standards of normal. Cowards wade in despair when our soul yearns to walk across the water. The miracle of faith dances with astonishing challenges and ecstasy explored to purge impurity and crystallize sincerity of intentions. I am sure you understand, as I do, that very few will ever understand the yearning in your heart and will consider the love I propose folly. The love I propose demands the acceptance of self and is in fact tasting the joy of me. Yes, it is mind boggling, but never the less accurate, to consider the embracing of forbidden pleasures as the solution to purge the impurities of neglect, despair and dissatisfaction in life. There are very few great accomplishments that were not originally forbidden by scholars and leaders relying on interpretation instead of revelation.

The primary principle of romance is love-making and love-making is the art of learning the motivation of her soul, heart and conscience. In comparison, great sex is knowing what to do without understanding the motivation behind the need or acknowledging the heartbeat of the soul. Perfecting the art of sex teaches us the benefit of multiple stimulation to produce exquisite orgasm in the physical realm. The exquisite orgasm will be way more than expected if you have never tasted the exquisite orgasm of lovemaking. I have introduced g-spot stimulators to influence squirting and still she will request or even plead for me to truly please her and the toy stays dry in the drawer. There is nothing more arousing when a man will commit to learning how to stimulate you spiritually, morally, emotionally, intellectually and absolutely physically with the coo of his presence. I am sure you realize, by now, we are not discussing fleeting relationships or one night stands. You must take the time to listen and observance character through her responses of multiple senses stimulation within experiences as the clue. The expression of heart of hearts references the motivation behind the physical need or even why we abstain from specific physical needs. My words in this journey is to advise the unseen of your motivation within the desire. In our youthful fitness we usually experience amazing sex when subjected to refined technique and even fall in love. As our appetite matures proper communication allows for your partner to intellectually, emotionally, morally and spiritually mature as well. The process of our amazing youthful sex to remain vibrant and transform into phenomenal love-making in compatible unison or even open compatible diversity is acceptance.

ALLAH! THE ALL

"The Principles of the Truth are Seven; he who knows these, understandingly, possesses the Magic Key before whose touch all the Doors of the Temple fly open" is attributed to The Kybalion. It proclaims three immutable laws and four mutable laws as the science of being. We are instructed in the importance of transcending the mutable laws as an innate power of humanity in achieving mastery. There are students of the Three Initiates who surmise the Law of Attraction runs through all seven of the Universal Laws. The Seven Laws are: Mentalism, Correspondence, Vibration, Polarity, Rhythm, Cause and Effect, and Gender.

I have already offered you a brief connection to these Seven Laws and I am not presenting them here to dispute their validity. I am your guidepost encouraging you to study and reach an intelligent conclusion for yourself. I actually want to elevate this conversation, leveraging the Seven Universal

Laws. It truly is about mastery if you are true in faith and this is unique to every individual soul. Our foundation is identical, but our circumstances are diverse. In the beginning, of procreation, thousands or millions of sperms competed to be the one selected and then it was established that Khalid A. Mustafa was The One and the remaining competition evolved into supporters or protectors of my success. They worked together to shield me from the elements, the Haters, focused on my demise. I arrived healthy, thanks to the protection of my supporters, ready to face the natural and manipulated challenges of the world.

Let there be Light... is an obligation on the truthful to share insights hidden in plain view. We cannot restrict the Originator of Creation to the Laws of Creation and expect to touch the higher meaning in the message. Our ability to think and rationalize does appear boundless, suggesting its mystery formed the idea of an Originator of Creation. We cannot validate, in any way, how the mind arrived into existence and that seems to be proof enough of its omnipotence. In my rational way of thinking, even before I ever heard the name Al-Islam, I believed there was Greater than what was being presented in religion. The Qur'anic Arabic language is complex and penetrating, which most likely explains my attraction to it. I am in search of the ultimate perception of bliss for me soul. I am not a scholar and I do not play one on TV, so I remain grounded as I travel the universe through the ability of my mind.

I offer you a reflection or vibration for your consideration and comprehend its connection to the way I love so intensely. The esoteric wisdom within the silent or hidden "AH" in The All influenced the demise of powerful kingdoms and their rulers, even though they possessed massive knowledge, power and control. We live within a manipulated design where materialistic accumulation rules, but nature will ultimately rebel and concur all the ideologies we adore. Our physical properties will perish and we have no clue to what is on the other side of our conscious or subconscious mind. Al-Islam offers us a framework towards understanding the Seven Laws of the Universe beyond materialistic prowess, in preparation for the hereafter. Materialistic prowess can be a change agent to the narrative, depending on how we leverage our success. The seductive and romantic properties of a healthy love is charming, kind, loyal, understanding, intriguing, honest and affectionate.

The Seven Universal Laws in Al-Islam are:

1.   Allah is The All

2.   Communication is offered through the wisdom of Al-Qur'aan

        a. Harmony of correspondence to our spiritual, moral, emotional, intellectual and physical self

3.   Vibration through the recitation, standing together in congregational prayer

4.   Duality is the binary foundation of our physical reality

5.   Polarity is the attraction grounded in the way it feels to us

6.   The cause and effect of our diet influencing health and the way we respond influencing what is possible

7.   Gender is about defined roles in social procreation of life

Al-Islam, is my organizing principle, as a basis for assigning value to knowledge pounding on my reasoning. It stabilizes the creed, of the learned, with sincerity in practicing what you know.

COMMUNICATION

You can take a breath now, relax your mind and kick back, as we glide into the aromatic cream of passion offered through my chime. Real Talk in the bonding of two souls, as a taste for what is to cum. The subject of our conversation is "Ache". I did not attempt to dress up the communication and offer it to your ears uncut.

B: *"I am needing you tonight as I do so many nights, feeling the absence of you inside me, and wishing I were with you in our bed. The sexperts call it a vaginal ache, and I am aching for you so badly.*

I am going to try and get some sleep to forget the feeling. Rest well, love."

A: "I am far from resting and more restless than anything else. I need you much more than you need me and I believe the sexperts call that blue balls. It is pushing midnight and I am up emailing you. I almost lost my composure this morning in class when a young sister sat in a chair and spread her legs and I knew it was me more than anything she intended. I took a moment to shake it off and focus on the content of the course.

I better rest before I am totally dysfunctional tomorrow."

B: "I drifted off to sleep not long after sending my email to you. I had to find some release. I whispered your name as I came alone in my bed, and then closed my eyes and fell asleep to dreams of a post-apocalyptic drama with very few staff onboard. I guess I am worried about the lay-offs. I am up working now.

Being up at this time has made me think that perhaps you shouldn't take me to the airport tomorrow. I can sleep on the plane, and then have a very low-key day ahead of me on Wednesday. You will have a full day ahead of you after an early morning getting me to the airport. I want you to get as much rest as possible so you will be ready for me Saturday morning. ;)

I love you, Khalid. I love who you are, the way your mind and heart works. I love the essence of who you are. Thank you for loving me."

B: *"It was so good to see you this morning. I appreciate your patience and the gift of your company. I can never seem to get enough of you. What is a sister to do?"*

A: *"Cum get some more...*

I can communicate with you with such ease and receive feedback on the important thoughts under consideration. I pray it is always that way, of you desiring me and enjoying my presence."

B: "It is almost impossible to decline your call, so...okay. Tomorrow.

If I ever felt a change coming where distance was growing between us, I would fight to bridge the gap and bring you closer. I am blessed to be the confidant of such an amazing soul."

A: "I believe it is so for us because we desire what the other offers naturally in intimacy. You fight to preserve what is precious to you and you must feel that your contribution is truly appreciated. You must be appreciated for who you are and not just for what I want out of the relationship. I love asking sometimes just for the pleasure of your response, but you offer me what I desire without a word flowing from my lips. I still cannot believe how hard my third leg becomes when you sit on my face. Who would have ever thought your ass on my face would be such a turn on? Being with you is such a joy and there is truly a distance when I do not see you in days. I try to get all the connections in within the brief time we are able to share together. I desire so much and am satisfied with you."

B: "It brings me happiness to know that you enjoy me. I wonder if you feel as turned on then as I do when I take you in fully, choking on your full length and girth. You are so delicious. I can feel my nipple getting hard now reminiscing.

I love responding to your ask and love even more anticipating your need.

I enjoyed every moment with you yesterday. I need a massage like that more often! You have so many talents. Insha'Allah, I will be blessed to spend my life discovering them all."

A: "Truth be told it took a moment for me to become comfortable watching you enjoy my third leg so completely. It was just beyond my comprehension that someone could really love me so completely and this drove me into an intellectual pause instead of enjoying the pleasing pleasure. My third leg experiencing the warmth and wetness of your lips as you gag while taking me in completely *is absolutely a turn on, yet observing your enjoyment takes the pleasure to another sphere of pleasing pleasure never imagined. The way it infuses a mind with manhood is extraordinary and self-control is essential to prevent from exploding immediately. However, I still have not decided which invitation I enjoy most between your warm wet mouth and your juicy hot pussy. I imagine having two third legs so I can experience both simultaneously and end up exploding immediately with the thought dancing on my brain. The way you enjoy me inside of you so much, tapping that G-Spot. Our last time together your haven was so wet my third leg was making slurping sounds as I rocked and I could see the white cream building at the base. I would love offering you my flavor of massage often and wish we had the time for me to offer you one of my full body treatments before caressing your insides in every way."*

B: "Since we are telling the truth, there was a point where I was very focused on doing "the things you are supposed to do" when I taste you. What I discovered was that some of those things didn't even turn you on, and I absolutely wanted to please you. I also was so focused on these kinds of supposed-to-do things that I was distracted from the passion and enjoyment of you. When I put away the supposed -to-do restraint and focused instead on your pleasure and mine, we both seem to enjoy ourselves so much more. My clit is tingling just thinking about your third leg. I don't think I can wait until tomorrow for release. The need is so intense.

I had no idea what it felt like to have my G-spot stimulated until you. The way you tap it with your third leg is just enough to send me over the edge. Once recently you used that stimulator from Good Vibrations, and it made me crazy (in a good way). I want to try it again, but without the vibration. That is just too much.

Yes, I hate the idea that I cannot have you inside me, so the need doubles when it is that time of the month. I cannot believe the level of physical intimacy we share, and I am so comfortable with you yet every moment promises a new adventure.

There is no reason to choose between one or the other. Whether it is having you deep in my throat or deep inside my wet pussy, it is all yours."

A: "This is a really special message you have given me here and I appreciate the love. It is critical to note that unfortunately my third leg can only be in one place, of your body, at a time and I must decide where to deliver my first squirt of cum. We are usually under time constraints and this adds to the complication of where and how. Yes, I absolutely believe you are all mine and the way you invite me in during that time of the month is so delightful. I love filling you in ways that soothes your desire of possessing my third leg. Oh, I am so hard right this moment.

I am so comfortable intimately with you that I just about try everything that comes to my mind and in that way there is always new adventures to experience. I could just flip you around all day making love to your whole body. Yes, that last tool, the purple wand, purchased from Good Vibrations is a winner of G-Spot intensity stimulation and I can still remember the expression on your face of pleasure to a plead for mercy. When I slide my third leg into your dripping, soaking wet pussy I usually cum immediately. It is an intense pleasure to know you are so wet and ready to receive me. We need more time!

I am reminded of Zane's book Purple Passion and I see the color purple is popular with toys that please women. Purple is a deeper hue of pink, which is the color that lines the inner walls of every women's haven. I wonder when a woman cum does the inner wall look closer to purple than pink? Yes, we need to play with the purple wand soon and I can observe you squirm with pleasure.

With you I learned early on that the supposed to do things where not enough and was just what my pleasure needed. I like to be and do things differently as a way of life. It still intrigues me how you naturally desire what pleases me and I observe your response change. The prime example in my mind at the moment is me sucking on your nose. The last time I did it you actually pushed your nose deeper into my mouth, whereas the first time you withdrew it in ambivalence. The supposed to routine is really what kills my desire and intimacy wanes. We should not be oblivious to the needs of the soul seek to please. If you cannot spark this form of seduction in love you are not with your true mate despite other compatibilities that bond the relationship. Yes, the supposed to do things are not my interest especially knowing everyone else is following this guidance."

B: "Yes, I cannot explain why it is that I am so turned on by what turns you on, but it is truly so. I remember these two times of you sucking my nose, and I have come now to desire it because I am coming to understand the emotion that fuels it.

I am really looking forward to seeing you tomorrow. We do need more time."

A: "Please enlighten me, because I cannot identify the impulse urging me and I am perplexed concerning the emotions that fuels the impulse *infusing the urge. I do not remember reading or hearing anywhere why such an impulse would surface doing such a moment of intimacy. It is like an admission and acknowledgement I would do anything to please you, because I know you do not desire anything outside of what my disposition will offer willingly. How can I know this?"*

INDULGE YOUR IMPULSES

I open with "Indulge Your Impulses", a poem worthy of standing independently as a message for those who can hear with more than their ear. However, love is forever evolving and maturing to enhance our mind towards possibility.

Touch me so that I know what it feels like to be alive

Hold me so that I know what passionate possession feels like

Confide in me so that I know what true trust looks like

Counsel me so that I know what it feels like to be understood

Pray with me so that I know what it feels like to submit to the Greater Love

Without you, it is easy to forget...

I adore you!

(This Love Note is worth repeating twice)

You are all that I have dreamt of, prayed for, and desired. It is my wish to give the same to you, bringing happiness to your heart's doorstep as you open the door to receive all that is yours. You are my closest confidant and surely my mind, body and soul call you by many names. For so long, I have been alone, waiting for you to share this journey with me. And what is a journey? For some it is simply an excursion, a moving from one place to another. But for us, there is always a deeper meaning. This journey, this passage through the stages of life, we were meant to travel these roads together. I have been stumbling along. My instincts repressed, my sight blinded by lack of truth, searching for salvation while lacking so much knowledge, trust, and faith. I am coming to understand who I truly am and life's true nature. You have pressed upon me the presence of duality and I have accepted that life is defined, in part, by challenge. I am coming to accept this, like the cool breeze after a spring shower or the storm that chases the lightening. I know now that with joy there is pain and I accept that this is a natural occurrence in life, and far different from the infliction of pain. Your love nourishes me and in so many ways, I am yours. Your heart should be at peace, knowing that it is at home with me. Allow me to love you for who you are in all ways and be free with me, knowing that you could never hurt me. If you believe that you inflict pain on those you claim to love the most, then you must not love me for you could never hurt me. I claimed your love a long time ago and you mine. Stay true to me in your heart and any pain that comes will bring the sweetest scent of happiness.

There will be many loves in our lives and rare will be the one who understands what we share. The board has been set many times, with all of the players in place and I have followed your moves and set many also, leaving others unaware of the greater plan at play. This is something we much bear individually and together. For my part, my intent was to love you and experience you, never to hurt another, as I sought to embrace Allah by embracing love. It is a difficult thing to deal in truth. It causes some to place blame unfairly an inappropriately, others to throw diversions, and still others to run. It is a difficult thing to deal in truth and while I have not yet perfected the craft, I am committed to seeking this and I would not have anything in its place.

Your life is a blessing to mine and to those who allow you to enter. Knowing you, really knowing you, is to commit to knowing oneself and not all are up to the experience. Live your life authentically and everyone, young and old, will not be able to escape what you lay *before them. In everything you do you teach and your focus is centered squarely on the love of the One True God. Stay your course, my love, with Allah, and the Angels will protect you always.*

LINGUAL TICKLE

Girls' High!!! The first year it became coed and long before being renamed Roxbury High School I was the only male inducted into the circle of leadership sisters. I remember Joanne (Joe, as we all in the circle called her), the first woman who required that I seduce and romance her without being under the influence of intoxication. She was strong and to the point kind of sister, who desired a man with natural self-confidence. She required me to man-up at thirteen and approach her as my Queen, if I was going to be in the business of seducing older women. I will never know her motivation or intent in educating a young mind, because a lessor male took her life for not giving him the time of day. Joe was my first clue that women desired more than a dildo pretending to be a man. The masculine handle for a strong, independent, self-directed women was common back in the day. It was a status of accomplishment within women gangs of the era and the Vine Street Gang was no different. We met at the senior's table for the sisters who ruled Girls High back in the day, through introductions of my cousin and her closest friend. Joe was such a beautiful woman internally and externally I just knew she was going to be mine the instant I touched her hand and gazed into her eyes. We often dipped from the party to walk in the moonlight and I would listen to her dreams of after graduation goals. She would even define the type of man she looked to marry, how many children she would birth and the career that would be her profession.

I cannot substantiate this hunch, but I believe Joe was indeed a frolic personality type. This paragraph is for you my love that never was and will always be mine. The irony within reality, symbolizing the unexplainable, is the wisdom cooing from every forbidden exploration offered to tease my passions. The frolic's personality loves with more intensity and with far more penetrating depth than any other soul on earth. The intriguing duality rests in the swiftness of evolving affections and infatuating twist of aphrodisiacs to tame sexual urges. I am smitten by your beauty, the sassiness of your sway and eloquence of your lingual tickle. The imagination of possibilities flourish through every fiber of your essence, as a youthfully vibrant woman of seventeen. The love tryst we shared acknowledged a certain right-to-life for each other, that illuminated our special connection. In reality I knew very little about Joe, except the depths of what rested in her heart and motivated her soul.

Love is an emotion, connected to a sense of strong affection and attachment. Based on its depth, love nurtures variety of complimentary feelings, states and attitudes of pleasure. Our deep, ineffable connection encompasses passionate desire and intimacy of romantic love to an intrinsic closeness of platonic expression. Our love is inclusive of a profound oneness and devotion of religious synergy. In other words, our love can always fill a basic need despite physical distance or even death. We are hopelessly each other's in this exploration of pure love. Within the essence of our shared pleasure of pleasing I am exclusively yours.

It is totally impossible to comprehend what I have done to be blessed with the love of such an amazing and wonderful woman. You are absolutely an edible fruit gracefully clinging to a flourishing exotic flower, blooming rays of happiness into my heart. It is my pleasure to please, as your halo, born to passionately explore delights reserved for bliss. My heart is yours, illuminating with every beat, causing life to flow abundantly through the essence of my soul. I am yours always in all ways. I enjoy you, adore you, and love being with you. A single essence of love shared across time and always unique.

Allow me to spit some school at you for a minute and offer you a view from the inside. Genuine soulmate lovers explore in awe of ecstasy, embracing the uninhabitable mysterious delights of sexual intimacy and entrust their body unconditionally for exquisite pleasures. Every soul's nature calls for a very specific and unique awakening, which the frolic's heart hears effortlessly. A woman can be in love with a man and completely committed to his happiness, until her heart wanes through neglect. Her heart will start to transmit a message, unconsciously emitting a vibration understood by the blessed few. It is an extemporaneous response to a yearning denied, that traditional moral convictions will plead with you to deny. The depth and breadth of the vibration will rise to the surface of the conscious mind. The woman in love transgresses to loving her partner and the soul is left waiting for the arrival of the frolic, as she aggressively attempts to enlighten her mate to the yearning of the soul. The good girl is evolving into a woman and temptation is caressing her libido. Unfortunately, her mate pleads for her to remain a good girl instead of supporting her maturity into a good woman. The seasoned frolic caresses the bad girl and good woman simultaneously in his instinctive way of encouraging and nurturing the best. The foolish hearted mind diligently tries to rationalize why his mate abandons a good life in search of great. He will ponder why she will willingly give completely to another while still loving him. He neglected to respond to the aura clues when her words fell on deaf ears. Her presence was screaming for attention and he never took a moment to hear the cooing. I listen without judging and earnestly focus to understand the gift of her words. The frolic is just the instrument willing to support the health of his lover without trying to own the destination of her love.

My mastery is in the attraction and seduction of woman who have transgressed from in love to love with their mate. To be brutally clear here, in 90% of the relationships sex and physical intimacy will never surface and it is like offering a virgin to her husband. The most delicate passions, for a frolic to navigate, is when the tryst in our soul exchange hearts and I am selected as the one. The frolic's temperament for a monogamous relationship deepens with freedom. It is the easy path to become complacent with our growth, suppressing self-realization and denying self-actualization to a point where we take for granted our spouse is doing the same. It is a contentment with illusion flourishing from an inner sense of what can be or reaching unintelligently into the abyss of darkness with conviction. The numeric symbol of the physical world is four, primarily because there is duality within light and duality within darkness. Darkness is not categorically evil, as light is not categorically good. There is a darkness the guides us into the light and a light that blinds us.

The focus of the darkness iterated here is a freedom to live with fearless passion of joy within the spiritual wisdom of completeness. It is not the darkness of evil and ill treatment justified through arrogance. The foundation of the light iterated here is sincerity of intentions. Possessing the heart is more than nurturing or tickling a passion for forbidden pleasures, we usually find expression in sex and define as love. Create a pattern of listening to your partner and let her know you are listening through actions for her to believe your words. You should never discard such a valuable treasure as futile or someone else will be nourished from the juices of the ripe fruit.

I can vividly remember the pattern of relationships throughout my life. From the age of ten until fifty I have heard the same words expressed in so many different ways of how special I am. In one way or another I have entered intimate relationships rescuing a rejected or neglected woman. I arrive as a protector and lover, offering of myself in ways never experienced. The relationship would be amazing and wonderful, full of words like "forever yours" or "everlasting love", until she realizes the courage and encouragement to be free. I am capable of offering and receiving exquisite love because I embrace intense pain to heal the soul of another. I will embrace your unsatisfied needs and unhappiness to fuel the uninhibited explorations we will taste. It is never my intent to possess the body or mind of a woman and this affords her power within freedom to act intelligently.

Pleasance is the active potential of power in a woman to be great, that cannot let go of what is expected. The nature of Pleasance is to come and go, as if on vacation, while remaining in her place. It still amazes me how many women birth children and still remain a virgin, never experiencing the art of love-making. Her body being used as an object of masturbation and neglected like the outdated toy. I am different for good reason and my purpose is divine of the worldly kind. Your haven is a precious pearl extending love and cradling life.

It all seemed to have started from lessons learned behind the Player's Club, from the prostitutes who decided to cultivate the ideal man. We both seemed to enjoy the reality of who I would become and the mark it would leave on my heart. I was cultivated as a protector and the ultimate pleasure in the art of love. It was extremely important to them that I possess unwavering authority, be deeply passionate and embrace women as a partner. The street taught me violence, the pimps taught me control and women taught me love. With all three of these lessons the principle foundation embedded on my soul is that who I am is not in the act, but the intent on my heart. Sex is an act that can be vulgar or a sacred gift depending on the intention of the heart. When copulation is offered as a gift I define it as a physical expression of lovemaking and when copulation is coveted for any underline animalistic aggression it is vulgar. Even when you indulge in copulation purely for procreation we are being cruel to the essence of our soul and we create life in the absence of lovemaking. In a society that encourages this caveman behavior, sometimes in very subtle ways, we embrace this ritual as manly in our youthful folly. Women will even come to expect it as an intrinsic male deformity and accept the abuse (even to the extent of experiencing pleasure) as permissible.

Lovemaking is about healing the heart towards self-actualization through pleasing pleasure. When a women's soul is deprived, yearning a signal of care, a mere touch can excite and cause her haven to secrete lubrication. The touch can be the right word in the right place at the right time. Orgasm is a result of freedom and relaxation within pleasure, accenting why so many women are deprived in the arms of a male. Understanding this delicate balance between intensity, stimulation and relaxation is the adjective of sexual performance. Lovemaking is this sexual performance intentionally pleasuring the heart and soul simultaneously. The Player's Club pimps counselled me in handling women to maintain control. It is very similar to how alpha men handle other men. There are circumstances, of course, where even the most aggressive woman appreciates being handled. I can still remember the response the first time I swooped down to pick up my wife, carry her through the door, down the stairs and into the car instead of watching her painfully hop along on crutches.

I am the secret that resonates behind your woman's eyes and allows her to tolerate all the shortcomings you provide. It is you she loves and my pleasures she adores. I am the intoxicant freeing her inhibitions and caressing her charm. It is not me you should despise, but the neglect distributed by your own hands and leaving her desires unchecked by exploration. I am still confounded at how a woman's heart can transition from being in love to loving and her man remains oblivious. Here are a few words for you to consider:

1.   Does she listen without hearing you, so you have to repeat yourself several times?
2.   Does she exhale (sigh of disgust) when you get close, but you never realized when she inhaled?
3.   Does she consistently close her eyes when you are intimate?

These are signs that you are the one, but not the one. The transition of emotional connection can be subtle or abrupt, but males tend to be oblivious to subtle change and usually caught by surprise when the shift is complete. It always amazes me to observe a woman's metamorphosis from helplessness through dependency to independence. I listen to the cry of her heart and respond as the guide she seeks. I nurture and cultivate the core of her essence (physically, emotionally, intellectually, morally and spiritually) to independence. I am her most cherished prize and will always possess what you can never claim. Simultaneously, I must gracefully accept being prejudicially dismissed unapologetically when the health of family can once again be prioritized. I will fill her void, encouraging her best and offering her freedom without hesitation. It is not a bond of bondage, but a bond in expression of who she yearns to be.

MELODIOUS CHIME

I lay on my stomach, my fingers tracing the carvings on the antique headboard. He was on his side facing me with his left hand resting on my ass.

He was drifting off to sleep now. I could hear the pace of his breathing slow to a calm place. I placed my hand on his arm, closed my eyes, and allowed myself to drift off to sleep with him. The room was so peaceful and still now...a far cry from where it was a few moments ago as our passions, held in check for far too long, were released in moans of pleasure on a hot, sticky Sunday morning. As I glance up admiring the rays of the sun reflecting off of the ceiling I reflect on my journey to this very second. As I exited the T Station, a brother did a double take and then said to me "Hello, Queen." It was very unexpected, and was followed by "You are just beautiful! Just beautiful!" He actually stopped walking and stood in his tracks while he said all of this. I slowed down, but kept moving, and thanked him over and over again. I was very surprised and pleased by his comments. The strange thing is, at that exact moment, I was thinking of you. Specifically, I was thinking of how it feels to make love to you. In that moment, I could feel your skin against mine, and your scent filled my nostrils. I was wet with thoughts of your third leg inside me.

Can you imagine that all of this exuded from me externally?! Wow! How wonderful.

I am missing you beyond belief, really in need of touching you. However, I am wary of waking your calm and stimulating your thirst for more than our bodies can secrete. It is amazing this hold you have over me, as I drift off imagining your fingers gripping my rear. It will soon be time for me to slip away and I already miss your presence at the thought. I cannot make my heart understand why this is so and I reach over to embrace us completely. The pain is overwhelming. Do you still feel this ever, or has time and familiarity given way to comfort and full acceptance? I whisper in the air how real the pain of missing you is and even at the thought tears gentle flow as a smile appears in knowing with every departure there will renewed arrival full of tension and passion reserved to cover me in cream. In the essence renewal our subconscious can manifest unconsciously. If I have neglected to mention this before I need you to understand that I am totally and absolutely

seduced by you. I mean that your entire being and
your desires and cares, these things all excite me.
They make me curious about you, interested to
learn more and to always be moving closer.

Self-Realization is an inward journey of reflection and analysis to annihilate the illusory identity ego of self and expose unrealized attributes of prosperity. This, of course, is very different from self-actualization, even though they both sway to the inevitability of our potential. Self-Actualization rises through specific actions taken to become better and is a lasting change in character. We can realize what change is needed and never possess the courage or strength to actually make the change. What we truly believe, under the many layers of deception we design protect ourselves, supports what we accept as possible. The awakening of self-realization is only a phase, no matter how spectacular, in accepting self. Acceptance is an act of contentment and never a position of complacency. I have accepted my role, embracing destiny and preparing for better with a prayer pleading for mercy, forgiveness and salvation. I am thankful for the fruit in hand, nourished by its nutrients and will plant the seed for a future harvest.

True Self-Actualization is a process that moves us through stages of development, while resolving our physiological needs at the foundation of our pyramid. The summit is merely an opportunity to observe what else is possible within the blessings of life and love. The authenticity of Frolic's creativity is playful, meaningful, sufficient and vital towards illuminating divine wisdom. We cannot ignore the importance Self-Realization in our journey or minimize the value of emotional maturity in the risk. We feel safe and secure in the comfort of the life we are familiar with, even as our soul yearns for a more fulfilling existence. Our soul is willing to swim joyfully in the turbulent waters of purposeful self-esteem. I am not promoting you to destroy the life of others in your care for some selfish pursuit in selfishness. I am promoting that you sincerely consider what is truly best for everyone in your care as a support for doing what is absolutely best for you. The vibration of love and belonging motivates us towards better. It is an amazing and wonderful adventure to observe such a metamorphosis, knowing the explorations will require the absorbing, dispersing and purging of pain to inhale pleasing pleasure. We are motivated through pain and pleasure, with pain reigning as the supreme motivator in embracing the ultimate level of Self-Actualization. We will act when the pain becomes too intense and will relax when comfortable.

The food we consume is a stimuli and is used sustain health or indulge an appetite. When we abuse the consumption of food we become obese or unhealthy. The relationships we form are an agreement to use each other as a stimulus to sustain health or indulge an appetite. We agree to use each other, with the expectation that we will not abuse each other in a healthy relationship. Intoxication is the abuse of a stimuli for a gain at the expense of another. If we acknowledge it or not the gain at the expense of another often includes an abuse of self. Masculinity is the mind used in a relationship to provide and protect, while femininity is the womb of mind used to support and comfort in a relationship. A male is not necessarily a man and a female is not necessarily a woman in a relation. Too often we observe males deflecting, rejecting and denying in a relationship where a man would request, accept and embrace. In the context of this conversation male is the intoxicating abuse of masculinity and is instrumental in the decay of male and female relationships. I may not be male, but I am a man.

Truth is a word in fact, yet our perception of the word truth is how we define it. There are many ways in which I can compel you to accept my perception of truth, that does not include the many ways in which I can convince you to accept my perception. The real mystery is when we comply without being compelled or convinced to accept my perception and we actually disagree with the perception of truth. The perceived benefit supersedes the perception of truth and we accept the fate of our circumstances as fact. We all dance in a balance of light and darkness; some define as shades of gray. I am however suggesting we all dance in a balance of darkness too, as well as a balance of light. We have all experienced where light has allowed us to see better and where the light blinded us. The evil of darkness is well publicized, where scripture defines darkness as a gateway into the light of vision and not blindness.

I am the darkness guiding you into the light and the light counseling you away from the evil of darkness. There is a duality in darkness and we all need a guide to discern between the two. It is usually when the darkness has submitted to the light do we realize the importance of its balance in healthy relationships. The energy from within the darkest recesses of your soul will fuel the fullness of your potential in the light. The purpose of the journey realized once I am purged of evil and the warmth of the sun comforts your soul. I am the darkness in your duality, extending an opportunity of purification with every temptation of the heart. In fear of the darkness you may neglect to refine a gem, forged through the friction of risk, in stroking temptation. The Guide's dominance as leadership must be relinquished so the divine purpose of the individual can flourish in unadulterated splendor. The gloomy darkness of black sparks fear and the sense of evil possession engulfing our self-identity is the perception. For the courageous the mysteriousness of black is full of potential and possibility. The restful emptiness inconspicuously shades our deepest and most intense emotions of forbiddingness and we are lured to taste the fruit shielded from the light of discovery. The dual role of black in culture suggests flight and discovery of an unknown truth. Black is authoritative and elegant, graciously inviting and aggressively pulling in the same motion. I am what you have been waiting for, fear most and the foundation of warnings guiding you to truth. Ascendancy is my nature, uniquely embellished to effect, as I allure your eye. I am not the source of your decay of demise, but am a decision of faith that must be proclaimed. I am the guidance of darkness vanishing in the light of a renewed soul.

I am the presence and perception of darkness enlightening your mind, heart and soul. I am the cooing vibration in your lobe soothing essence and rejoicing in your joy. I am the mind is search of his wolf, seeking adventures to claim the divine. The womb ready, willing and capable of roaming the earth as a wolf is designed to be mine. The wolf who can erect her man with exquisite pleasures and devour his nutrients to infuse the soil for the future. The wolf is a bad girl, but a good woman and a cat is a good girl, but a bad woman. The good girl that is a good woman is considered a kitten and the bad girl that is a bad woman is considered masculine. The good girl is inclined to baby her boys and raise her daughters. The male conditioned to lean on the good girl is doubly crippled. He neglects to build the required strength in the singular leg limb of the "Y" chromosome. There is an instinctive sense that speaks from the unseen, marking where we are and pointing us towards a goal. The guidance offered here is not for everyone and still you must pass it forward.

I am reminded of a cartoon picture of a man giving a selection of animals an opportunity to fairly compete, by giving them the exact same opportunity. The animals included an array of land, water and air creatures. The opportunity was to climb a tree and the winner takes all. Can you imagine the expression on the fish? When there is an irreconcilable incompatibility for opportunity within a relationship equality is not an equitable solution. The souls in a relationship should complement the other in a useful way and support the success embedded in the relationship. It is the activation of two souls resonating on the same hymn without compromise to their innate frequency.

Please excuse the digression before I dip into the last part of my prose, orating experiences and communications from back in the day. In the prurient exposure of same gender explorations, I am to clarify my position on homosexuality. I cast an infatic "no" in support or encouraging of homosexuality. In my era, during my initial exposure to women making love, it was never perceived as an act of homosexuality and I embraced this understanding. I embraced this understanding, without questioning, because I cannot recollect knowing a woman who was sexually active with woman only. I could not imagine, talking about naïve, a woman not desiring a man or a man sexually desiring a man. However, I surmise our ignorance cultivated the sexual climate we are experiencing today. What is permissible was always manipulated to benefit the male appetite to possess. The purging awarded me, in writing this book, is my bridge into a renewed perception of reality and acceptance of love in my life. I am sharing the collective explorations of thought and experiences in designing a message for those with an ear to hear. In my journey I have learned to love myself, uniquely, in a way no other can and in that discovery I have learned to love you better in my journey of pleasing pleasure. See you in the future, when you get here.

THE TACTILE TRYST

During The Heights of the seventh month

Marked by The Night Journey on the seventeenth

The Spirits of seventy-two submits to The Truth

*Arriving on the twenty seventh odd evening of the
Sacred Month*

*We are consumed with thoughts of The Night of
Power*

What is a human to do?

I am tantalized through your seduction

Wooed within the romance of your love

Touched by the grip of your aroma

What is a mind to do?

I am drawn to the place of your naming

Waiting to be embraced by the gaze of your eyes

The sensations of passion flows through my soul

I sense the beauty of your presence

It is the blessed month of your birth

The moment of the day draws nigh

What is a man to do?

The graceful aging in time offers us a decade
within a moment

The melody of your voice coos my name

My appetite for a taste of your nectar dances on
my palate

You offer me the pleasing pleasure of your
pleasure pleasing nature

The delightfully enchanting sweetness of your lips

What is a soul to do?

I am yours to quench the thirst of your desires

The bovine mature female offering sustenance
with practical guidance

The two mystical characters of wisdom

Hearing the woman who pleads for justice

You should be mine!

Figure 4 Barrington Edwards - Artist

PART THREE - PASSION

TENTH & OLIVE

There are moments and experiences in your life that change things forever. Tenth and Olive was one of those experiences that set in motion destinations I never imagined, that continuously evolve as love continues to flourish in my life. The way you love others is truly reflective of the way you love yourself and determines the way relationships will be solidified in your life. The way we communicate within relationships is to reveal or conceal an essential essence of who we are at the core of our conscience. In a point of time Tenth and Olive was the crossroad that led to everything progressive in a city determined to thrive once it could design a plan to survive. It is a lesson to my life to never give up, regardless of how ugly circumstances can become. We can only witness the experience from our perspective and that becomes our reality. When we take a moment to pause our opinion and listen to others define the same experience, we realize the identical fact is multi-dimensional and never flat in defining truth.

Changing the narrative of your life starts with changing what consumes your thoughts on a daily basis. When you take a moment to reflect it is ironic how much energy is given to concerns more than possibility. If negative thoughts like fear of poverty, fear of failure or fear of illness consumes us we can be driven and accomplish milestones those who are paralyzed by these same fears deem impossible. When we observe someone who has earned material success, we are confused when they live a destructive life of drugs and abuse. They will pretend their accumulation of things is a source of true happiness, but when you examine the details another story unfolds. The medium of mass media will even try to convince you that these destructive patterns of living is the reward of success and declare it freedom of choice. However, when you examine the success of a life driven to accomplish, even if we disagree with their purpose, you will usually discover a very different pattern of success. We must conduct a thorough examination of our narrative to frame passions that motivate us. The more penetrating question is what passions cause demise when success seemed self-evident. When we consider pleasure as a passion in contrast to our passion niche we identify very different motivators influencing behavior.

We must always consider the motivations that drives our passions not connected to our personality niche. It is my contention that sexual intimacy should be an expression of lovemaking, that rewards us with procreation. Of course, we can experience sexual intimacy without copulation and we consider it foreplay or after play, depending on your preference. When I was a youth, hanging out behind the Player's Club, one of the lessons the sisters taught me was the sin of masturbation. In their perspective, especially in a male just reaching puberty, release should be a gift offered by a women or a wet dream resulting from the touch of a woman. Masturbation deflates your need for sexual intimacy and deforms your ability to attract, seduce and romance women. Women can sense your sexual energy and this naturally stimulates conversations touching intimacy.

Part three is a collection of actual experiences and actual script that was exchanged in written communication with multiple individuals. It is my intent to keep the content to as close to the original as possible to maintain the purity of the exchange. Passion is the explicit expression of desires and fantasies as a process of maintaining and nurturing intimacy. I am a very passionate soul, adoring my main expression and loving variety to feel complete. I have discovered the ultimate value in a woman openly revealing her deepest fantasies, without a concern of your manhood being threatened. The risqué of seduction and romance is the naughtiness that fuels authentic passion and authentic communication for the pleasing pleasure of pleasure pleasing. In the rhythm of the "Momma, What's Funkadelic" I echo "If you will suck my soul I will lick your funky emotions."

The liberties I possess, in touching and tasting your body, arrive in a carriage of seduction, with a canopy of romance. You are absolutely breathe taking as an intelligent, sexy and vibrant lady. I am blessed to have you as mine in so many exquisite ways. When I am handling my business properly, in my professional life, I focus on what pleases you. I imagine squeezing the firmness of your ass as your juices drip, sending sensations though my body as your nipples hardens between my lips. Anticipating the warmth of your lips tantalizing my senses or me slowly entering your juicy haven. My words find its place and I hear your response, emphasizing you have read my message three times. Each read leaving you breathless, wet and wanting to make love to me.

Reading your response has made me think about what it takes for me to find someone irresistible. I love that you are so many firsts for me, and that, despite my inexperience, I have a sense now of what I need and enjoy through us. It is, though, hard to separate what I really need from what I have come to need through us, or maybe there is no difference...

I have a serious dilemma. My sexual appetite is just on the rise and I am craving serious sexual activity

several times a day, sometimes finding myself
preoccupied with cravings.

While I am pretty sure that this is all related to my
being a woman in her 40s it is making me feel a
little dirty (especially when I resort to watching
videos), and not in a good way. This preoccupation
and the sheer physical need for intense sexual
encounters makes me feel lust full (at least, I think
it is lust, but I am reading to learn more), and not in
control of my own emotions. We know I hate the
latter, and the former...I don't think I have ever felt
quite this way before. Of course, you always
awaken something special inside me, but that
combined with the intensity and frequency of the
need is new to me.

 So, the feeling-a-little-dirty part just brings to the
surface all of the ways I have been conditioned as a
female, to think about myself in relation to sex.
Once you add, on top of that, how we are
conditioned as women of faith it is just unavoidable
that I would feel guilt. I am trying to let go of the
double-standard teachings I received in my youth

about sex as a female, while trying to understand the way we are conditioned as women of faith, while wanting to obey Allah, while trying to accept my own humanness. These things are so in conflict that they make my head hurt, and I can see all of the ways that I have disordered my life. For example, if I were married to my soulmate, I would eliminate several pieces of the conflict, but the choices I made very early in life and continue to make now (even though they are for good reasons) put me right in the middle of a spiritual, physical, mental, emotional, and moral conflict. If it weren't so frustrating and disturbing it would be laughable.

Yes, I feel you, baby. I was reflecting earlier this morning on how deeply you possess me. Even when I am engaged in self-pleasure the moment belongs to you, and your name slides off my tongue in a whisper of ecstasy. I am so much yours it is unimaginable to conceive of a life without you.

I am drawn to this email as I sit here to pen you a few scripts of prose. It is important for me to express that pleasing you is my pleasure and this automatically includes ways beyond what I can provide as an individual. With the right third I contemplate the extra pleasure in the mix and can never forget how dripping wet you were while watching me make love to another woman. Your response influenced me to consider the heights of pleasure you would achieve with two delicious third legs pleasing you simultaneously and filling you with sweet cum. Yes, it is absolutely about the right third or our goal in the pleasure of pleasing is incomplete. I always desire to be in the mix, as we add flavor to the exploration of pleasing pleasure. Can you feel me, baby?

I cannot disregard anything you extend, even when it is done accidentally. It is important for me to never underestimate the value in a gesture. Kitten extended me the gift of her letter (loving words) and cufflinks as an expression of her love. As humans, if we neglect to consciously honor the intentions behind a gift we usually take it for granted and can even unconsciously believe it is part of a debt owed. It is so easy to be selfish and never truly value a gift in a way that the giver would truly appreciate. You have enhanced this consideration or sensitivity of properly honoring a gift in me and to explore the deeper value than the surface act.

The picture you sent me of the two sisters lightly embracing nude had a surface value I commented on and a deeper message that intrigued me, requiring a much longer comment. However, you captured my thoughts in an expression of "Just acknowledging the power of such an intimate act with you." The way you love to love me is supreme and breathtaking in so many ways. There is such a pleasure in me observing and knowing you are being loved (sexual intimacy) properly by another, especially a woman. The main pleasure is that a woman offers sexual intimacy qualities I cannot and adds to the pleasure we both can deliver for you at the same time. The circle of pleasing pleasure, pleasure pleasing, we share is absolutely amazing to state the least. Your pleasure increases my pleasure and my pleasure increases your pleasure until we are pleasurably exhausted until our next dance. I think often on the depths we would share if we were blessed with three days of quality time together in some exotic location in a penthouse suite overlooking a city or a villa on a great mountain overlooking a waterfall. Can you feel me, baby? I adore you!!!

What you have said about never taking a gift for granted is so right, and I need to do better about this. I don't know how I have enhanced this attention to giving for you. As I experience you, you have always excel in this area.

The imagery that you have expressed in response to my comments confirms how well we understand each other, and I find myself reading that email over and over again, wooed anew each time. I try not to read too much into my observations and at the same time I do not want to underestimate the value offered. It was not a question of sincerity in the gesture, but more of a realization that this is real serious for her and I have to consciously honor the gift. Of course, this always causes me to reflect on us and how I can be better for you. I am pleased I can offer you so much pleasure and still I thirst to offer you more. You honor me in ways never imagined and your magnificent soul touches my heart of hearts. When I reflect on the way you make love to me and offer your body so completely to my whims I know your words are true.

The idea of the walls erected to protect your heart crumbling at my feet is a sign of your submission. The suggestion that your heart pounds to the rhythm of my possession is a sign of your devotion. The imagery of the depth and breadth of your love acknowledging my third leg as a scepter is overwhelming. I must and should be a guidepost directing you towards Allah. It is essential that I respect such a special gift, always be grateful and never take you for granted. I stand between your thighs, grasping your ankles and gazing into your eyes as my scepter stimulates the province of you haven. Your warm juices bathe me with pleasure, as I glance down to witness your white cream flow joyfully. You motivate me towards greatness and I am in service to your seductive pleasing pleasure. It is Allah who has given so much despite ourselves and He alone is our Lord of all the worlds or systems of wisdom. What a disgrace for me to be alone without you in my arms tonight. It is the balance for the forbidden love we share in the darkness of worldly responsibility. I adore you!

I would think this to be a sincere gesture. So much about what she has said and done in the past is consistent with this giving.

You always make me feel loved, and I never feel taken for granted. Sometimes distance grows between us on the most superficial levels of emotional connection like when time passes between moments of physical intimacy or when one of us is facing a very full schedule, but we are always connected on a much deeper level as is the case with soul mates, and we find ways to bring the two of us back to us. When you make love to me my soul intertwines with yours, and sometimes I worry that it is all in my head, some tendency I have to over romanticize, but then you gaze into my eyes, and our souls speak a language all their own, and I know you are mine, and any walls around my heart crumble at your feet. My mind stirs in wonder at how I am not wrapped in your arms every day since my heart is pounding to the rhythm of your possession.

So, no, you are not taking me for granted. If anything, I must constantly assess that I am not taking you for granted and that I am loving you properly. Your hedgehog will not allow you to dwell in a state of ignorance as you have demonstrated even by the email below. You absolutely possess my love, and you seem to love me better with every stroke of your pen on paper, your fingertips across the keyboard, your scepter against my G-spot, your magnificent mind and soul across my still actualizing ones. You are always propelling me closer to Allah.

Now, after reflecting on us, and on what it is like to love and be loved by you, my body aches to be with you, and I must end this email in a state of suffering not so easily soothed in your absence.

I do not need to negotiate for what is rightfully mine, baby. The romantic in me loves the foreplay instead of the thug approach. Once we are in the moment I can hit it like a thug or then rhyme to my swag all in the same dance.

Words can only express so much as to what one feels for another. My words will be brief & soft spoken. The light and energy you have shared with me is more long-lasting, fulfilling and desirable than any kiss, stare, hug and passionate sex love-making I've experienced. These words are for you.

You!!!

Shortness of breath

Blood rushes

Warmth overtakes me

My soul begins to sing

Nipples harden

Clitoris tingles

My brain whizzes

A smile starts inside and grows

Wet panties

Warm heart

Mind in motion

My soul takes flight

Happiness.

It is You.

You are an amazing man. No one makes me understand what is really important in life the way you do. I don't know how to not love you. I was made to love you. And look what you have done for me?! Look how you have enriched my life, and brought me back from being so lost. Pleasing you, beyond the joy I receive, is a way to honor not just what you have given to me, but who you are. When

I give to you I am honoring the wholeness of who you are, I am thanking Allah for His creation, I am acknowledging the beauty of self -determination in action. To know you is to love you.

ARRIVE FOR A TASTE

B: You were delicious this morning... you made my morning. Fell asleep last night after climaxing and calling your name. Had to change the sheets.

A: The seducer is seduced...

I will keep my mouth shut in the future.

B: How will I slip my nipple into your mouth if you keep it closed?

A: There are always exceptions...

Did your colleague visit your hotel room last night?

B: Yes! She noticed my nipples were hard and asked to come in. Once the door closed she kissed me and made her way to my nipples. Slowly she made her way to my clit and I fell back across the bed. The

warmth and wetness of her lips and tongue caused
me to cum hard. As I laid there panting she stood
up and undressed. Her firm chocolate nipples stood
at attention and I could see the moisture on the
hair of her pussy. I reached over for me G-Vibrator
and slid it between her thighs. She moaned as it slid
over her g-spot and I rocked it lightly. Ditashia fell
on top of me in the bed and kissed me violently.

All we needed was you...

There are those moments when lovemaking
transforms into animalistic fucking. She walks
through the door dripping wet with anticipation
and foreplay is not required. She is ready to ride,
releasing it all for pure delight. Addressing the ache
of needing me inside, immediately, I hit it hard and
fast until she screams "fuck me baby" and then
leans over to whispers in my ear "I will have a taste
a little later", as I continue to wield my magic leg.

FUNXION FUN

The best way infuse passion is with fun and the most seductive and romantic fun is fantasy moisten with explorations of forbidden explorations dear to your lady. In writing I love to mix experiences with fantasies to forge a picture of what is blooming internally. I often follow an experience with written communication or a verbal conversation connecting to the value tasted through the experience. The exchange guides me into the next selective experience to build our bond. I find woman, or the human nature itself, wants to be expressive and safe. When we cannot embrace the balance between the two that stimulates the greatest joy the darkness of our nature explores alternative solutions forged in pain. The passionate display of anger is a balance for a flaw in our character that we can justifiably transfer onto another. The aware soul embraces this duality and searches for the joy in the way we respond to the darkness and especially the evil intent that surfaces. It is healthy to step into the light, without swaying so sharply to become enlighten through the purity of sincere intentions.

It is Monday afternoon and I pick up the telephone to dial your number. Your voice dances in my heart through the fiber optic lines, as you answer on the third ring. I pause to hear your breathing before responding. We talk for about forty-five minutes and you inform me of a conference you will be attending in Washington, DC. It is a four-day conference and you will be leaving Tuesday evening and returning Sunday morning. The early morning workshops are mandatory and the Saturday evening dinner highly recommended. There will be an array of presentations, awards and recognitions by business leaders and our county's politicians. Yes, you will be recognized for your excellent work in the community and representing your team receiving an award.

I listen intently and congratulate you on being an amazing and wonderful woman. We exchange a few emails between Monday evening and Tuesday afternoon, as your way of providing me with as much detail as possible. It is your way of including me in your life and allowing me to be part of the experience in your success. I receive the final text before you board the plane and I know you will be faced with a very business schedule once you arrive. I am so happy for you and start thinking of the many ways to show my appreciation.

It is late Thursday afternoon, as you sit for dinner with a few close colleagues, at the Ruth's Chris Steak House, for a tasty meal. You order the signature T-bone steak with asparagus and rice. You pick up the full-flavored prime cut and savor the taste, as the juices excite your palate, while fantasizing on inhaling my third leg. You glance over the table to see one of your colleagues gazing at you with tempting eyes. You have become close to this native DC sister and she reminds you a lot of Berry with a pinch move firmness of form. Your panties become instantly wet and she smiles invitingly. In that instance your cell vibrates as an email from me reaches your inbox.

I received a contract offer from a major IT company and I needed to attend a strategy meeting in Washington. I was in DC checking into the Four Seasons, compliments of All Covered and their associates. As you glance down to read my message Whitney keenly watches as your nipples harden beneath your sheer evening dress. The Four Seasons is a great way to experience Washington. *"What could be better than staying at the Four Seasons Hotel Washington for the weekend? Perhaps arriving to your spacious and beautifully appointed room to find a welcome note and a mouth-watering seasonal amenity, or waking up to a sumptuous breakfast every morning, delivered right to your room, or savoring it in Seasons restaurant. Create a weekend of cultural pursuits, sights and shopping to explore all the nation's capital has to offer, including unique cultural events, world-class museums and historic monuments. All of this with the ease of our overnight valet parking and late check-out. Now that's the perfect recipe for a great weekend."*

Washington is legendary for its shortage of good men and woman getting together to please one is a standard modus operand for sexy woman. Team sport cultivates much more action than trying to score solo. Whitney has a sense for these opportunities and knows instinctively you are about to meet a maintenance man for a booty call. She was already attracted to you and now the excitement was boiling as her panties became soaked with sticky juices. As you all exit the restaurant she stands very close in order for you to inhale her aroma. It did not take long for Whitney to get you alone and invite herself to your room. It was obvious she understood and wanted to add her specialty to the pleasure.

The connection was obvious and Whitney decided to make her move, with a whisper of seduction in your ear. The invitation was exhilarating, but tonight was yours and you would consider other explorations at a later time. She would not leave without a taste to demonstrate her aim to please and afterwards offering a passionate kiss. You jumped into the shower and started preparing my dessert. You knew sharing your exploit with Whitney, at the right moment, would send me into overdrive with excitement. The idea of us having three evenings together and multiple opportunities during the day to experience the town is truly a treat.

You retrieve the card from the concierge and take the elevator to the Capital Suite. I am reading the first edition of the Honey magazine to keep up on what is happening with a sista. I am waiting in my silk underwear, with Basil aromatherapy scenting the air and some old school Luther playing softly in the background. This will be our twenty-four hours, locked away from our usual interruptions or schedules. I took the liberty of purchasing a few new toys and replicating some of the ones we have in Boston. The door shuts and you pause in the luxuriously large room and the treat awaiting you. Slowing you undress, dancing exotically cooing sensual phrases of passion. Posing nude, you toss your panties into my face. I inhale the aroma of your juices and watch your every move.

My patience is rewarded with a lap dance and I reframe from touching you with my hands. Without warning I wrap the blue silk scarf around your neck and pull firmly. Your nipples become super hard with excitement. I gaze into your eyes and smile. You are reminded of Whitney and her skill at eating your pussy excites you even more. You grip my third leg firmly, with intensified pressure until I let go of the scarf. You lean over and take me into your mouth, until the tips of your lips are touching my balls. You are relishing ever gag and inhale for maximum penetration deep into your throat. I explode into your mouth and you swallow every drop. I throw you over my shoulder and carry you into the bedroom. I toss you into the king size bed and watch your tits bounce in the air. I take the time to lick your juices from the inner wall of your thighs and from around the lips of your gorgeous pussy. Fully lubricated I insert my index finger deep into your ass and start to pump it as I lick the clit. You are finally able to focus on us and block out all distractions. I grasp your hips, lifting them from the bed, to insert my firm dick slowly into your moist pussy. I start to rock your hips and pump hard with mine to plunge deep as possible. I flip you over on the bed and you are now on top, riding me cowgirl style.

You take this opportunity to offer the details about Whitney and I grow firmer with every word. Yet, your excitement overshadows mine as you explode, Cumming all over me, with passionate intensity. You continue to ride and I message your clit with one of the vibrators. Exhausted, you fall to the bed and we embrace in sticky juices. The evening is young and Barry White is grooving us with "Can't Get Enough of Your Love", as we consider another exploration. We will soon make our way into the shower and began again dripping wet. We wash every inch of each other's body and you tell me more about Whitney.

I drop you off at your hotel room so you can prepare for the conference day. We plan to meet for lunch and connect after your dinner with colleagues. It is a day of intense negotiations over the details of the contract and I am ready for the challenge. If everything goes well I will be visiting DC often and this will be the chance for us on the regular. One of the partners, Robert, has become my greatest ally in the whole process and we are really connecting. He is about fifteen years younger than me, chocolate brown, with a muscular physique. Robert is very sharp mentally, dresses sharp and considers me a mentor on a diversity of topics. We get together after the meeting to debrief and sharp talk future plans. Robert is in the Potomac Suite of the same hotel. I glance at my watch, taking note I have about an hour before we connect for the evening. We are in conversation as we step into my suite so I can grab something.

When we step in, you are posing nude and decide to ask "who is your friend?" Robert's eye lights up with excitement and is obviously growing an erection. What a surprise for both of us and an exploration Robert will never forget. He can see the shock of surprise on my face and knows this was not planned. You step closer to Robert and introduce yourself. As he shakes your hand you use the other to unzip his pants. His flow of words stammer as you grip his dick saluting. I sit back in the easy chair to watch the scene unfold. As his pants drop to his ankle you drop to your knees. It is a strange feeling watching you swallow and work him in and out of your mouth. Your skills are amazing to observe and still I am uncomfortable, for the first time, watching another man's cum fill your mouth. Tonight you will please and be pleased by two, experimenting with those fantasies you keep safely locked away.

As I lean against the pillow I watch you peacefully rest with a slight smile of expression. What thoughts are swimming through your mind is my thought of contemplation. We are always considering how we will merge the best pleasures in our life to experience an even greater pleasure. It is not what you do, but the depth and breadth of the connection with the one you experience it with. The mere brush of your body against mine is tantalizing and awakens my anticipation. I need to shift our focus to think about task, obligations and responsibilities or our primary purpose for being here will be forgotten. The company, All Covered, has a table at the Saturday dinner for the conference and invited me to attend. This will be my opportunity to dress to impress and meet Whitney. It will be our last evening together before returning to Boston and we must find a way to accent special in every exploration together. We have already decided to attend the Love Club over the Zanzibar Club or the 9:30 Club because of the luxurious private lounges for some public sex explorations after some wild dance floor moves. We did stop at FunXion for a healthy lunch and correct aphrodisiac. It is ironic how we handle business comes down to the way we play as a celebration of success. The business culture recruits the characteristics it needs to forge success and that shines through our personality more than anything we can wear to impress.

I was walking down the street, passing an outside bar, where four women were sitting. The first sister reached out her hand and lightly grasped mine as she looked me straight in the eye and offered small talk. Of course, a brother has to pause at such an invitation. She then asked if I wanted to play penis ring. They had a plastic penis with plastic rings and I thought smooth with a gentlemanly smile. With the ease of comfort, I responded, looking her directly in the eye, I only play with my own penis. In the spirit of play, to bring the other three sisters into the conversation, as I offered each eye contact. I simple suggested that if they offered me to play ring the pussy I would accept their offer. The sister second from the end blurted out yes, before the dominate sister took control of the flow. She suggested if I played penis ring they would be open to ring the pussy. I seductively repeated my statement and started to walk away. The bartender, who was silently observing, commented on my great response and ability to hold my stand as the man in this play. My response stated I was down to deliver if this was more than just a game.

CELTICS NIGHT

"We are two rows from the court, chilling in leather seats and conversing with the stars." The preceding sentence is abstracted from the text, of a forbidden lover's tryst, taking place on the evening of a Celtics championship game night. The intimate and connecting details, originally in this chapter, would create the perfect storm, in at least five relationships, at first glance and spread like a virus. The content infringement is removed and liberating content included, accenting the complexity of love, shared as an overwrite just before print.

My dearest Khalid, I miss you so much. I know I made a stupid, dumb decision. I need you in my life. It is not fair to you, that I pretend I don't care. Yes, I'm hurting, but it only hurts more when I'm not around you. When I feel like I'm losing you. I am truly sorry. I know I hurt you, but at the time I thought it was the right thing to do. My life has become somewhat empty without you. Sounds strange, huh. How does the saying go? "You never know how much you need something until it is gone." Whoever created that saying must have felt the way I'm feeling. I miss you and need you in my life. We were great together and still can. I want to work on a better relationship with you. I know we have much to work out. We'll get through it. The end result will be truly amazing!

I am writing this letter to you, to express how I feel about you. I need to tell you some things I feel you need to know. We have a great deal of history together. We've been through a lot. Your new ring tone, "You made me love you" is truly how I feel. While this may be true I have grown to love you like I never loved any man before. I fought us for so long. I fought fate. I denied the love. I need you back in my life. Let's build!

I'll work on my communication. I'll make a better effort at coming to see you. I told myself I was going to keep this letter about you and I. I'll work on giving you what you need. You deserve better too. We can be that for each other. I know we can.

We have to work together. Stop avoiding each other. Express our feelings more. You know our minds and with the deep emotions it can get real serious. I love you. I miss you. I need you and want you. Yes, I can want you. Most of all I love you!

I have never heard such devotion and amorous words, from her lips, until this annotation to who we are for each other. I was shocked and humbled by the honesty, within the realization of possessing a heart. The words and more importantly the meaning supporting her words underline why proper communication is essential with sincerity. It is so easy to destroy or deform the most precious gift you can receive in life. I have been working for decades on how to be more thoughtful with love and respecting the essence of a soul willing to yield her heart. In some paradoxical way I believe writing this prose is to examine my sense of feeling undeserving of such love. Words cannot define what is possible through purity within sincerity of intentions, that the glow in a woman's eye can instantly.

CACAO SNOW CRYSTAL

Birth

My eyes open

Given a chosen name

Preserving your souls living enzymes

Offering a luscious chocolate hue

The scrumptious taste on my tongue

Caressing with delight

Awed by your piousness

Blessed through your rightly guided heart

Your curves counsel me with pleasure

I whisper into the breeze of the winter night

Awakening the thinker in you

Cooing between snow crystals illuminating your beauty

Dance with me

Dancing in the snow

Who you are pure and unique

Harmonizing with each crystal

Gliding from the sky

Your flavor is unforgettable

Cacao Snow Crystal of mine

Yearning for another taste of mine

Tapping a uvula rhyme

Music to our ears

Erecting to the sky

Pausing between your thighs

Waiting for the sign

Tantalizing shaved chime

Dew dripping too

Me and you dancing in the snow

Cooling our Cacao view

Feeling you

Thankful eyes of mine, witnessing the love that is mine

SEXUAL TITILLATION

My lips form a suction halo around your mound and I tickle your inner walls with a breath of air, eliciting elevation in sexual arousal, I will hold that position until your body tenses with excitement. I will then start to make a circular motion with my tongue, as I caress your perineum, until your juices squirt into my mouth. Your thighs will quiver in delight while I suck on your erect clit. The flow of your cum will explode as a volcanic eruption, just before your muscles go limp with submissive pleasure. I sit up on the edge of the bed to bask in the moment of offering you joys never to be experienced with another. The urge to lay my head on your bosom and simple inhale the exquisite aroma rising from your body is soon replaced with me slowly working my lips across your body. Pausing between your thighs I will taste your nectar oozing onto the sheets. Lubricating my index with your juices I rock it over your G to awaken your body. I return home with only your dark chocolate nectar sauce to savor for the evening.

I often talk about the power and impact of duality, but who would have ever imagined you would be my ultimate extreme compelling indulgence. You are the most illicit exploration and the purest love I have ever experienced. I cannot imagine discovering anything else even close to what we share. You allowed so much of what I need and desired effortlessly to create happiness that has alluded me all my life. Sweet dreams, chasing the demons away. I adore you!

I would never want to leave you hard and craving release. Next time, come over and let me to enjoy wrapping my lips around you. I will savor the taste of your sweetness in my mouth until it blankets me like a lotion made just for me. That first plunge that you have promised will feel so good. It has been so long and I am warm and tight and waiting for you. Just the sight of you erect and ready will get my juices flowing immediately and I will be unable to delay that first stroke, anticipating the sensations that only arrive when you are inside me, home, where you belong.

I can't stop thinking about you. I fall asleep imagining your arms wrapped around me after a passionate session of lovemaking involving lotions and oils, candles, vibrators, succulent fruits, rich caramel and chocolate sauces and a scarf (or two). The taste of you lingers on my tongue and I enjoy the feel of stress rolling away as your body relaxes next to mine and you drift off to sleep. I awaken aroused and wanting more, but find myself alone with only my fantasies.

I have already resorted to self-pleasure once this morning. I believe there will be a second time soon as my mind naturally turns to you when I am naked and wet in a steaming hot shower. Each drop of water caresses a different curve and I imagine which curves your hands would trace if you were with me.

Your words created a flood of memories possessing my mind as the yearning to taste you rose in my throat. The image of your succulent nude body standing there wet, calling my name, brings me to an immediate erection. I sit here harder than a concrete column, only desiring you and the pleasures we can experience together. I visualize the scarf tease, musing that evening like it was a moment ago and excites a zeal to explore more. I need to fuck you right now! When your period prohibits me from entering, I bend you over and flip you around to temper the frenzy of violating the code. Sliding my erection between your breast and circling its head around the areola of your nipple serves as foreplay before landing home. As the period arrived, so must it subside, as a sign it is pipe cleaning time. Plunging fiercely to remove all grime, in a way that is claiming what is mine. Your ecstasy purr signs on the line, testifying with the sound.

I am wet now just thinking about it...

You and I created this supreme love. We created it, without hesitation, within a forbidden exploration anchored on the most exquisite pleasure pleasing possible between two souls. We didn't just fall into

it the way people fall in love. We made a conscious
choice to love each other deeply, honestly, and
completely. You are my closest friend, my lover, my
guide, my confidant. I love you wholeheartedly.
You made my body do things I didn't know it could
do and your sensuality mesmerizes me.

We did create this supreme love intentionally and
we wanted each other in ways no other could
possess. We forged the kind of love we wanted to
receive and give, as an exploration of self-
actualization. We now stand in the crossroad of
this supreme love and destiny, facing off with
responsibility and principle. With trust and
acceptance, we formed a bond of unimaginable
freedom that social norms shun and religious
dogma expels. What is a wonderful and amazing
woman, like you, to do with such a discovery?

The physical action we took is the manifestation of
all the purity within and it exploded our sentiments
into an elevated realm of pleasure we can never
again deny exist. The rational response is to never
pass the signpost of spiritual unison. The act will

knock down your door of resistance and nothing else will matter. The risk of it all is truly considered an intellectual disaster in reasoning and still it is the absolute best decision that can be made for a courageous soul demanding freedom. I understand the struggle waging within and I am praying for your success. You now have what you have always wanted and it is in direct conflict with the responsibilities of your present reality. We see through our perspective and that is our reality, unless we are willing to position our direction to witness a different perspective and evolve who we are into refreshed reality.

The pleasing pleasure of wholehearted love is ours and it evolves regardless of what we do from this point forward. We could never physically see each other again in this life and what we share will continue to evolve. We plead to discover balance and reframe from indulgence, yet the inner walls of your love haven is screaming to feel me pulsate within, as your juices flow to cover my third leg. I yearn to feel your lips grasp my leg, until it is hard and you summons me to flip you over. Your beautifully resolute cheeks, exclusively mine, inviting me in. The thrill of the pain and pleasure causes your nipples to harden, as you gasp the sheets, waiting for me to enter. Whatever you desire the most I am willing to extend freely as we sway with dominance and submission for the ultimate expression of our supreme love. What we have is very special and very few would understand why we became to be.

The joy of our explorations and mutual self-actualization reigns unparalleled over the challenges embedded in the duality of our fleeting life. We were blessed to move our relationship from the attention of physical delights to secure spiritual actualization and this is a cause for rejoice. The mystic essence of reality is pure and divine, looming high above the worldly passions of sexual expression. The pursuit is to suffuse your spirit with the love, memories and fire reserved for me. We must relinquish one conscience of perception as we are born into the illumination of another. I embrace the darkness in order to see correctly in the light. Observe the sacrifice made for every great accomplishment and we will see the folly in clinging to the standards of normal. Where others wade in despair I stand in harm's way, for a cause greater than myself. Our penetrating conversation excites us and I spread your thighs wide to enter you one more time.

SEXUAL ABSENCE

The sensation tickles my toes, as my third leg slowly parts your chocolate thighs and moves smoothly into your hot haven. I can feel the warmth of your juices massaging my third leg, passionately inviting me in. I surrender to your every whim, with a delicious spin. In the calmness of our harmonious groove I command you to ride. I demand for you to ride me harder and faster, as the sweat begins to form on your skin. The wetness falls to my body like dew in its morning glory. It is the way we seal the lingering taste that never fades. I watch as your body begins pulsating with ecstasy, while admiring the firmness of your nipples waving to me in the air. Just before you collapse in exhaustion, I push you back onto the pillow in order to return the favor. I start to ride you hard, determined to tame a wild passion ready to be owned by her King. I grip your body to plunge deeper and the thrust compels you to scream "FUCK ME! FUCK ME, BABY! FUCK ME! I AM YOURS!"

The mounting fluids oozing from your haven, moisturizing your body, invites me to insert my finger. I can feel your boy arching to welcome me, knowing my tapping and adding pressure from the rear ignites the flow of your cream. I flip you over to enter your haven from the rear, enjoying the view as your round exquisite cheeks smile, when I part them. I can feel my erection passing across your G and hitting the inner walls of your stomach, as your hips move vigorously, owning the glory. Covered in your cream I carry you into the shower and take careful consideration in cleaning every inch of your precious form. With every centimeter clean and glowing I rest you on the floor in front of the fireplace. The heat from the flame dries the water droplets from you skin and compliments the warmth you feel inside. We embrace for a long time, in silence, before you begin to whisper one of your darkest fantasies in my ear. What the words revealed I will never share, as our marriage vow.

This is our way, in the lapse of time. I often believe your absence is intentionally design, defining the intensity rising over time. The way your body gives, to me, ignites this instantaneous energy that moves through us when I enter your haven for the first time. Creating a continuous exploration, evolving the identity of what we share. The pure delight, of anticipation, in diving deeply between your thighs or gazing as you grip to guide. Where most women will sneak a taste of their nectar, you wash your cream clean orally. The sticky cream protein erupting is my contribution for your delight. Sexual passions subdued, we commence to nurturing the soul when cuddling. I marvel in the miracle of our intimate communication and the breadth we are willing to share in the depths of exploration. Your voice and ideas excite me with hours of spiritual, moral and intellectual pleasures. The meaning in the message of your words stimulating levels of emotional intimacy never obtained with another.

NUBIAN VIOLET

You are on my mind, once again. I awoke with the need to touch you, as my thoughts drifted into the reality of our circumstances. This dream that stirred my soul, seemed real, as it captures so much of who we are. It is a craving for a reality that does not walk with the forbidden explorations of our life. The willingness to feel your breath on my face or hear you snoring in my ear, as you fall asleep beside me is the favors deferred. I will massage your muscles until you coo with a smile of pleasure. In that moment I will gentle kiss the tip of your nose and lick the curves of your lips to express the affection in my heart for my exotic flower.

In this journey of struggle and turmoil I stopped under a tree for shade. While resting my head against its body the blossoming tree gracefully released a fruit to fall into my arms. I looked up to witness, for the first time, branches full of flowers waving in the breeze. I glanced downward to behold the splendor of the exotic fruit in the palm of my hand. I closed my eyes to consider the splendorous flower birthing such a scrumptious fruit. Like a sudden flash of brilliance, I realized that there is a time to merely enjoy the view and a time to taste the juices of ripeness. The nutrients nourish the soul and feeds your life force. With every flower and fruit offering itself, I must careful select which to claim as mine and respect the purpose of them all at the same time. The purpose of plenty is never to release your life force into every fruit that wobbles or approach the flower, in your possession, without explicit consent. The flowers watch to witness, as the fruit encourages accuracy. I always take excellent notes. I remember everything exactly as I remember it.

I am home early from a day at the office. Heading straight for the bathroom I turn on the shower and detour into the living room to kick on some jazz. I pause for a minute to calculate how much time I will have before you arrive. Slowly I return to the bathroom to strip myself nude. Stepping into the hot shower water I can feel my muscles relax immediately. Your name glides from my lips as I smile to myself. I take special care in washing the stain of the day from my body. I select the herbal cleanser you favor to grace my presence and cover myself with the essence. I rinse myself squeaky clean and shut off the water. I dry myself quickly and step into my most tantalizing briefs. Entering the kitchen, I start my ritual of preparation and seafood is on the menu.

I will create a salad of freshly chopped organic vegetables, with a splash of tropical fruits and bathed in chunks of crab meat. I am compelled to sprinkle the salad with a variety of organic berries.

Yes, this will go perfectly with our main course of lobster claws, chopped into exquisitely seasoned portions, and slightly steamed oysters. The long grain wild rice is embellished with organic lentil pea sprouts. Asparagus is diced into unnoticeable bits to add the special touch in tantalizing your senses to the seafood broth soup. I reach into the cabinet for my secret blend of organic aphrodisiac herbs to season the meal. It is time to set the table and mellow the music out just a little bit more. We always set the antique dining table with our finest china, crystal and silverware for every meal. It is the way we signature that every moment is special when you are dining with your soul mate. The mood is never complete without the proper aromatherapy tempting the appetite and strategically placing African Violet petals throughout the house. I set the home made cider to chill in the middle of the table, just in case we need to wet our palate.

I crack the front door, to make sure you experience no resistance entering our abode. I hear your car door shut, as I am putting the final touches to the dinner plates. I rush to greet you, with a small chunk of warmly rich fudge between my fingers. You enter cautiously, wondering why the door is open and knowing I usually at work. Your eyes widen, as they excitedly come to rest on my briefs. Placing the chunk of fudge between your lips I hang up your coat and I remove your shoes. We embrace for what seems like eternity and we start to kiss. Your lips are warm and the temperature of your tongue is elevating. A sign you are turned on and the evening as only began. Your senses are overwhelmed by the ambiance of the room. Your whisper "I love you" into my ear as you nibble on the lobe.

I work my kisses, nibbles and licks around your lips thrusting my tongue deep into your throat as a treat. Slowly and rhythmically I caress you neck and head with my lips and tongue. Your hands move across my body sensing the desire you arouse within me. I remove your jacket to unbutton your blouse and reach around your body to unleash your firm breast from the bra. They stand erect looking at me as the nipples start to harden. Starting from the top right breast and holding the left in my hand I start to kiss it so lightly. You take the liberty to remove your skirt and panties as I press my body against yours and my tongue starts to move downward heading for the hairy mound dripping with wetness. Your knees start to bind as I lift you up and place your exquisite rear on the edge of the dining room table. My lips find your clitoris standing firm, your legs parting as you place them around my neck. I look up into your closed eyes and say "shall we proceed?" for them to open, with glittering joy wooing so softly the confirmation in your mind. I proceed to suck as my finger massages the G and your legs grip my neck as the climax builds deep inside you. Soon you will release the first of multiple orgasms for the evening. This will be our night, breezes through my mind, as you lean back knocking the dishes to the floor.

The crashing of china pushes me into consciousness and tears roll from the corner of my eyes in the face of reality. I am wide awake now and your essence still clings to me in your absence. The pleasure of pleasing and the pleasing pleasure we share is the blooming exploration extending beyond the boundaries obligations to drench us with joy. It is the elevated sensation of home within my soul, living as a marvel for all time. You have completed me in so many ways and in that same breath you are the forbidden fruit ripe to claim as mine. I cannot drift back sleep, with the image of my dream so heavily on my mind. I restlessly toss in the bed, noticing an African Violet pedal on the pillar. The vibrations of your absence is calling for you to be mine.

I can hear Pleasance in the background and see Berry in my presence, with Blossom on my mind. You are the 3some on my mind, claiming my time. The deepening love of one infuses the depth of love for the other and is equally shared as a circle of love. We understand the other through every syllable sound, tasting the cream combined. I adore the amazing woman in you and proclaim publically you deserve better than the obligations presently chaining your chime.

MOTHER'S DAY

The alarm rings as the clock strikes midnight and Pleasance kisses you good morning. Berry kisses Pleasance and then kisses you too. A penthouse tryst away from motherhood obligations and family responsibilities. It is not often you are able to take these Yoni Retreats for a little womanly love. I am here to serve. All of the cooking, preparing, cleaning and pampering is mine for the pleasure of three. The crystal bell chimes, as a request for my presence. You request for me to prepare my purple asparagus, marinated in honey, aphrodisiac dish. I spread the dish across the body of Pleasance, for Berry and Blossom to enjoy. While you taste and chat I prepare the Jacuzzi and make sure the temperature of the shower is just right. You each shower before stepping into the Jacuzzi and start to massage the oils over the skin of each other. I am attending to the cleaning of the bedroom and the preparing of what you will wear today. You will, at least, need three different outfits to accommodate the adventures of the day.

It was the Mother Day's Gala last night and a request to pause at Peter Parley to enjoy a walk in the park, as I complied as your chuffer. I watched the three of you slow dance together under the stars of the evening. The Gala was part of day two for the Yoni Retreat and being served by males, as you serviced each other. The selecting, cleansing, meditating over and inserting the egg was part of the first day ritual. The egg massaging the inner walls of your haven as you walked or danced. I observed as the stress and challenges of life evaporated into the air and your embraced the essence of womanhood. You learn so much about correctly caring for a woman in observing how a woman cares for herself and requires in the way she receives care.

I believe it was this specific Gala I first met the sister I define as Bloom. She would embrace other woman firmly, yet gently for what seemed like an over extended amount of time in allowing the transfer of energy decide. I listened to her convey, in detail, the personality traits of the woman from the energy exchange. It was then, once confirmed as accurate, that she would recommend the Yoni eggs necessary to balance the spirit. The correct harvesting and forming of eggs carry its own benefit in the process of healing. Bloom taught me that there is an essential role in this process for the male purged of impurities and properly sensitized to the energy life force of the womb. When I reached that balance she chose me to insert the Yoni of fertility and soon after her first child was born.

Bloom continuously emphasizes the importance of your woman feeling protected, relaxed, safe and free in your presence to release the full pleasures of her essence. Too many males have tasted the body of their woman, without every coming close to possessing the heart and soul of her essence. I have been blessed to even refine my presence to receive the heart and soul of a woman's essence without every indulging in the sweetness of her nectar flowing down her thigh. It is my intent to counsel as a guide, knowing the youthfulness of my prime is finally on a decline. The manly motivation to obtain shifts in wisdom to retain, as I still maintain discretion in my palm. The ultimate lesson of Bloom was in observing her embrace a woman for the very first time and secure a trust that is usually formed over time. In letting her to explore a woman's body in a way she cannot explore her own a connection is solidified. Within hours Bloom would have the woman orgasming and even squirting, sometimes for the very first time.

I witness this identical freedom between Pleasance, Berry and Blossom. Watching them intimately play with each other before moving to the bed from the Jacuzzi. I can hear them giggling and moaning with pleasure as I clean the bathroom. They each encourage the other to touch, kiss and lick what their male partner neglects. The chime of the crystal bell beckons and I stand in the doorway of the bedroom, waiting for the next request. You ignore me to torture and increase the intensity of tension as I watch in silence. You form a circle to taste each other, as you rock the vibrating vibrator across the G. You request that I lubricate and pass you and Pleasance a strap-on. Berry is on her back and Pleasance mounts her. You mount Pleasance from the rear and you both start to rock in harmony. You ask me for guidance, in order to stroke like a man. Berry thrust her hips forward for Pleasance to enter her deeper. I do not know why watching a woman fuck another is turning me on. You would think sisters not needing me would have the reverse influence. However, I understanding what most men or even lesbians do not about the usage of dildos. The weapon of martyrs to the rescue is the only hint I will provide.

You dismount Pleasance and you change positions. With Pleasance on top I watch her caramel ass gyrate in the air, as she hits you with everything over and over again. I think she is enjoying being the man a little too much, but who am I to complain. As if Berry can sense the erection growing in my pants, she tilts her head and winks at me. With the cue you demand that I strip nude and I stand there firmly grasping my third leg. The torture seems to go on for eternity, as I watch the three shades of beauty entwined before me. You stop and cast the strap-on to the floor and three of you line up and bend over the edge of the bed. I take turns, swiftly moving from one to the other, as you demanded. My third leg is drenched in the cream from all three. It is all a little too intense for Pleasance, who has never come close to so many orgasms in one evening of lovemaking. She excuses herself, taking a shower, before heading to the other bedroom to rest. You watch me ride Berry, as her cream around the base of my third leg.

It is obvious to me you are yearning to taste some pussy and lick every drop of her juices off of my third leg. We want so much of the same for the other and this evening will be for you. Berry wants you so and obediently moves gracefully with your every word. Berry's pleasure is in pleasing you and intuitively desiring your desires. Your passion to please me is her passion and Berry asks you for guidance. This is your opportunity to coach and observe, as you recline and coo directions. Berry follows without hesitation and I am gazing at you in total excitement. I aggressively flip Berry over and enter her slowly before picking up my rhythm with force and speed. Berry's juices are dripping wet all over me and the bed. My third leg is saturated with her juices and rock hard, when Berry drops to her knees to wrap her lips around my third leg and taking me deeply into her mouth. Watching the pleasure in your eyes as you observe Berry work my third leg throws me over the edge and I explode.

With a mouth full of my cream Berry turns to kiss you, working her way across your breast and down to your moist haven. Your thighs part magically, so she can easily taste you. The thought of Berry moving from me to you is adding to your excitement, as you savor the taste of my cream, deposited by Berry. You enjoy seeing me stroke my third leg deep into her mouth and haven, as the pressure builds within. Berry works her tongue around your clit and caresses your G with the tip. Watching her work brings me to attention and Berry screams when I enter her from the behind. My eyes meet yours and lock in mutual consent, as I hit that ass to the beat of your heart. Reaching around I strap the well lubricated dildo onto Berry so she can fuck you. My force causes the strap-on to slide swiftly into yours. The vibrations of my motion flows through Berry's body, as your ass shifts with each thrust, to elevate the delight.

The three of us orgasm in sync and you lick me clean of Berry's cream. The sounds of pleasure glides from between your lips and awakens

Pleasance in the other room. We are satisfied and still yearning for more, as Pleasance enters with a smile. The joy in her eyes is only a sign of the divine. We focus our attention to pleasing Pleasance, by kissing her lips, nibbling her nipples and sucking her clit at the same time. Our hands move across her body as we taste her with our tongue. It is not long, before her cream arrives while releasing a howl. We are all licking the cream from her inner thighs, waiting for it to subside. We head to the shower, before they rest together in front of the fireplace with a little jazz sound.

Figure 5 Double Happiness

Subconscious Conscience

PLEASANCE BLOOMING

As a young boy wandering the streets of Boston I always demonstrated the courage to take what I wanted when being denied what I needed. The paradox of my reality pushed me to imagine the irresistible and embrace the joy of adventure. The sisters in the life took pride in schooling the future, with wisdom reserved for the few. One lesson was how to watch for the sexual burning in the eyes of a woman and determining how much of its flame is for me. I truly enjoy the dance and the excitement of anticipation with every sway of a woman's body. The charm of a real man tantalizes exquisitely, when he can hear the calling of her body and move in rhythm with the vibrations. I will taste the fruit of your deepest and innate idiosyncrasies without hesitation, as your ultimate love elixir.

I will explore the intimate boundaries of your essence, inhaling the wonderful aroma of the ambiance, as the temperature of your firm thighs raising between your firm thighs, luring me for more. It is an absolute joy to caress the curves of your body and watch it respond to my touch. The moisture between your legs anticipates a downpour, for us to bath in vigor, as your muscles quiver. You whisper my talent is a powerful aphrodisiac. I move, vibrate and pulsate at the speed and intensity desired with movements that move you. Geisha Balls inserted, my tongue works to send soothing sensations through your body. I continuously roll you over to tease every inch and keeping the Geisha in motion. My mind is entertained with memories of how you would find a reason to casually brush against me unnoticed. I would envision this moment of you lying across the bed, legs wide open.

I gently trace my finger across your body. Moving from the top of your forehead, between your breasts, to gently open the lips of your haven. Your body begins to vibrate uncontrollably, as I remove the Geisha Balls and work the small Je Joue vibrator around the gorgeous surface of your protruding lips. With a dip of my finger I slide it through the sticky juices and insert it slowly. Oh! How you jiggle with pleasure, with multiple points of stimulation, as you cream all over the sheets. I quickly flip you over, to behold the most exquisite ass. You are truly a blessed woman. I hear you moan and exhale in excitement as I start to lick, bite and slide my tongue between the cheeks, traveling all the way to the base of your neck. With a move of careful consideration my erect third leg enters, as your ass rotates to receive me. You beg me to go deeper, as you spread your legs. I pin your arms down, as you wiggle in pleasure. I arch my back to deliver a thrust for the deepest penetration.

We retreat to a warm shower where we soap each other and rinse off. You take special care in cleaning my third leg, before you start to moisturize it with your tongue and kiss me softly all over. My body quivers with pleasure as I form the hardest erection ever, within your firm grasp. You whisper in my ear to please fuck you. I lift you up as you wrap your legs around me and I carry you outside into the moonlight dripping wet. You lock your legs around my neck, leaning over the railing, as I taste your juices and caress your beast. The tension and excitement intensifies as you whisper for me to fuck you once again. I take your hands in mine, removing them from the tight grip of my hair, swinging you around I bend you over the Liberator and bound your limbs. Playing with the upper inner walls, I place the head of third leg in your haven, as you wave you ass vigorously for me to go deeper. I continue to tease as your cream builds and streams down the shaft of my third leg. Finally, you scream "FUCK ME!" and I reply with a full thrust of penetration to ride you as I would to tame a wild stallion. We get lost in time, as dawn peeks over the darkness, with you nutting in rapid succession.

The blood rushes forward as you press my prostate gland to gain even more mass. I unbound your limbs and you turn to push me over onto my back. You grasp my firm erection, soaking wet with your juices, and commence to licking it with fierce lust. Your tongue explores every inch, as you include my balls into the pleasure. Without hesitation your mouth consumes my third leg, as I hear you gag for air and observe you refusing to let go for a second. Your eyes call for me, as your mouth stays busy, to shoot my load. I let you work it like a lollipop before I explode, as cream fills you mouth and runs from the corner of your lips. With a suction motion you inhale for the cream to flow down your throat. I giggle as my scrotum massages your chin and the suction of your lips tickles my shaft. As a skilled practitioner, you feast over every drop, digesting the liquid as if through a straw. I cream a second time, as you squeeze the base of my rod, before I start to lose form and my lips find you heaving and waiting breast. I nibble your nipples, squeezing them between my teeth.

Subconscious Conscience

BERRY BLOOMING

Shortness of breath, blood rushes, warmth overtakes me, my soul begins to sing, nipples harden, clitoris tingles, my brain whizzes, a smile starts inside and grows, wet panties, warm heart, mind in motion, my soul takes flight and happiness flows. It is you!

We did intentionally create this supreme love and craved each other in ways no other could possess. We offered the love we needed to receive and self-actualization is the reward. The trust and acceptance we fertilized sealed a bond of unimaginable freedom. A freedom that social norms shun and religious dogma expels. You are an amazing and wonderful woman always ripe for naughty delights. The decades of exploration discovery we share appear less than a year. I still smile and lick my lips, visualizing our first tryst cruising down the Interstate, with you tasting me the whole time.

I can't believe you thought I was embellishing how much I enjoy tasting you! That would be so out of line with who we are...for me to fake something like that with you. I absolutely love pleasing you that way. I have mentioned this before, but sometimes I just want to stand back (okay, lay close) and look at your third leg, or work him with my hands, or my mouth, or ride...so many options for ways to enjoy him. Mmmm....let's talk about something else.

The physical exploration expression we share is the manifestation of all the purity of our love within, exploding to release impurities and elevating us into a realm of pleasure we will never again deny. It was you who guided me to Pleasance and I who guided Pleasance to you. Vanilla Pleasance remains the dream deferred, waiting proper nurturing in our circle of love, dancing our way to an invigorating vanilla success. The endearing lust she possessed for you, you possessed for me and I possessed for her, is the summit of what shall be. The intensity of endearing lust shared was too much to entertain in the same bed at once. The intensifying force of delivering more and being better never subsided in the moment of pleasing pleasure, until our bodies collapsed in total exhaustion. We would wake hours later, literally stuck together with dried juices from cream and sweat. The irony, if we dare call it one, is that the wholeheartedness pleasing pleasure of our love is forever evolving, regardless of what we do from this moment forward. Whatever you desire the most I am willing to extend freely as we sway with dominance and submission for the ultimate expression of our supreme love. Our love is an indulgence in joy, completeness and awareness every soul should know.

For so long, I have been alone, waiting for you to share this journey with me. And what is a journey? For some it is simply an excursion, a moving from one place to another. But for us, there is always a deeper meaning. This journey, our passage through the stages of life, we were meant to travel these roads together. I have been stumbling along. My instincts repressed, my sight blinded by lack of truth, searching for salvation while lacking so much knowledge, trust, and faith. I am coming to understand who I truly am and life's true nature. You have pressed upon me the presence of duality and I have accepted that life is defined, in part, by challenge. I am coming to accept this, like the cool breeze after a spring shower or the storm that chases the lightening. I know now that with joy there is pain and I accept that this is a natural occurrence in life, and far different from the infliction of pain. Your love nourishes me and in so many ways, I am yours. Your heart should be at peace, knowing that it is at home with me. Allow me to love you for who you are in all ways and be free with me, knowing that you could never hurt me. If you believe that you inflict pain on those you claim to love the most, then you must not love me for you could never hurt me. I claimed your love a long time ago and you mine. Stay true to me in your heart and any pain that comes will bring the sweetest scent of happiness.

There will be many loves in our lives and rare will be the one who understands what we share. The board has been set many times, with all of the players in place and I have followed your moves and set many also, leaving others unaware of the greater plan at play. This is something we much bear individually and together. For my part, my intent was to love you and experience you, never to hurt another, as I sought to embrace Allah by embracing love. It is a difficult thing to deal in truth. It causes some to place blame unfairly an inappropriately, others to throw diversions, and still others to run. It is a difficult thing to deal in truth and while I have not yet perfected the craft, I am committed to seeking this and I would not have anything in its place.

Your life is a blessing to mine and to those who allow you to enter. Knowing you, really knowing you, is to commit to knowing oneself and not all are up to the experience. Live your life authentically and everyone, young and old, will not be able to escape what you lay before them.

It seems I left my panties there. That was so careless of me!

Subconscious Conscience

BLOSSOM BLOOMING

Passionate attraction is such an enthralling covetousness and enslaving desire, known to dismiss boundaries when unchecked by conscience. It howls for an uncontrollable compulsion to actualize fantasies. I beckon you to talk more about your affection for Kitten and you honor my invitation. Kitten is for you and I have only enjoyed the view. I realize, accept and appreciate your desire to taste such a sassy and sexy bronze flavored sister as I observe your tongue explore the depths of her wet haven. The emotional charge we share ignites intense desires and uncharted passions between you two. The scrumptious lure of her nectar parts the hymen of her haven and you impetuously lick the cream flowing towards the path leading between the oval cheeks of her ass. I love to watch your body explore the cusp of delights that has you all aquiver. With unrestrained and unrestricted explorations your labium swells to reveal a firm, succulent and tasty clitoris.

As Kitten tenderly caresses your chocolate skin crescendo viscerally the strokes tantalizes your essence and warmth illuminates as euphoria lubricates your mind. Watching your voluptuous body sway excites my palate for a taste of your orgasmic liquid, filled with Oxytocin, calling me from between your thighs. You are the perfect aphrodisiac for Kitten, inciting her lips to engorge and areola to darken, as the blood rushing through her veins broadcasting excitement. My flaccid leg stands erect, in full girth, as I focus on the cream dripping from your haven and the cunnilingus being performed. Kitten and I erupt simultaneously and I can hear you sigh with satisfaction. The egg and sperm birthing your offered the world the most exquisite form of beauty a man can behold and is now perfectly decorated with the intertwined bronze complexion of Kitten's frame. You groove together smoothly, as a single cell, segmenting as a pair when you come up for air. The bright rays of light, illuminating through the pane, reflects off your tasty rear, gyrating rhythmically, letting us know an orgasm is near.

The two of you explore the intimate joy, as I enjoy your joy. When the two of you awake I am gone, like a vision in the night disappearing in the light. I instinctively know that your afterglow of your delight is not my right. However, it is not long before my cell vibrates and your words whispers in my ear. "I can't stop thinking about you." I fall asleep imagining the lovemaking as I am wrapped in your arms. Lovemaking embracing lotions and oils, candles, vibrators, succulent fruits, rich

caramel and chocolate sauces and a scarf or
two. The taste for you lingers on my tongue and I
anticipate seeing you one more time. I awaken
aroused and resort to self-pleasure just before
piecing the steam for a shower. Each drop of water
caresses a tense curve of my muscles and
rejuvenates the vigor of my core. The Kitten text
reads, "Thank you, for being a supportive audience.
Come claim what is yours anytime. Take care. "

SHANTE

We walk into the second training session of the
first day for a three-day workshop, titled "The
Intrinsic Connection of Souls", discussing the
content of our first training session for Talent
Management. The soft, yet authoritative voice
invites us in and we both sense the identical
sensation of excitement simultaneously. We glance
at each other and gaze back to our next presenter.
I immediately start to flip through my agenda to
see how many training sessions Shante would be

presenting, over the next three days, of six training sessions daily.

We are a stone's throw away from South Beach looking to bring back valuable insight to improve the operations of our agency. The weather is warm to hot, but the breeze was cool to the skin. The workshops where taking place downtown in the luxury of the Mandarin Oriental Miami Hotel and our suites where in the Setai Hotel, offering adventure beyond the training. The possibilities have my mind swimming with ideas, in leveraging the opportunity. I start to formalize activities for the nocturnal nature of my personality

I listened with strict attention to every word that danced from those full lips, taking detailed notes to construct the most penetrating question I could ask to stimulate the deepest possible connection, speaking directly to the heart of her soul. I gazed into her shining brown eyes, synergizing with the passion beneath the professional delivery of the subject. Blossom allowed her leg to rest against mine, seeing 3some written all over my face, as she introduced herself and complimented the insight shared. Of course, I had waited to the very end, as closing remarks were being made, to ask my very complex question deliberately full of insightful conclusions to draw interest.

I approached her and was immediately swooned with urges of sexual fantasies, as the word "Clive" whispered audibly from my lips. Shante's eyes lit with amazement and I had her attention. Her body language shifted, becoming more receptive to casual conversation. I asked if it was possible for Blossom and I could talk with her later, about the question I asked and some of the other thoughts related to her presentation. Shante smiled slightly, understanding the clue immediately, stepping closer to us. Shante agreed to meet us in the Azul Restaurant at 8:00pm, joking about her inability to sleep at night. B.E.D., BLUE and Cameo came to my mind immediately. Oh yes, Shante was wearing the fragrance of Clive Christian's Imperial Majesty and I could hear her body calling our name. I believe my unique blend of Sandalwood stirred her senses a little as well.

Each of us arrived promptly at the restaurant dressed casually with a slight flare of sexuality. We were providing a little eye candy for the other and you must be particularly careful not to overdress for the Miami nightlife. We took the first evening to really get to know each other, test the boundaries and teasing. It was a pure treat of amazement to watch Shante's nipples grow firm under the silk dress that clinked to her breast, as our conversation would turn seductively playful throughout the evening. We even danced before retiring for the evening, as so many eyes watch me with these two very sexy and charming women. I barely got one foot in the suite door before Blossom literally tackled me, tearing off my clothes. I returned the intensity by hitting it seriously that night. In the early dawn hours we discussed our strategy towards a 3some with Shante.

Around 7:00am, while Blossom was showering, the suite's telephone ranged. The voice sweetly asked, after I said good morning, "is Blossom there with you?" I replied with "yes!" knowing who's voice I was listening to. She replied, "Good! I am looking forward to seeing you both for breakfast." When Blossom walked out of the shower, I tossed her onto the bed, devouring that haven, until her juices where all over my face. We both showered again and she took that opportunity to taste me before going making our way to breakfast. On the way, I told her about the telephone call from Shante and we laughed with delight. The breakfast was very professional and there was no need to test if Shante would be down for a little double taste, since her early morning call said it all.

That evening we met at the BLUE nightclub and talked about visiting B.E.D. However, on our last evening together we went straight to Blossom's Suite, after shopping for all the appropriate accessories needed for an evening of sexual indulgence of exquisite pleasure. What happened that evening will remain as the foundation of all that followed. Shante had never been with another woman, but always wanted the experience. She talked candidly, of why she believed Blossom was the one. Blossom talked about her experience and some of the explorations that just never evolved.

We agreed that I would only observe until requested.

I weaved in affectionate name whispering, with their rhythmic moans, to intensify the intimacy. Playfully, I commented how sweet and juicy they both looked and stressed my anticipation of a taste. We left the BLUE early and went back to my suite, to move this forward a little quicker, with the required privacy needed. We both watch as Shante slowly undressed and started revealing the real beauty hidden by the clothes. Shante's smooth skin was chocolate brown fudge and I could taste the succulent moistness in the air. Her body frame was very similar to the beauty standing near her, as I admired both. Her long locks draped over her shoulders touching the top of her firm breast. Breast almost identical in size and firmness to Blossom's, with protruding nipples. We all showered together and I got into something comfortable, before taking my seat in the easy chair. When she turned to approach Blossom, sitting on the bed, I could see her cheeks sway with each step. They allowed me to get relaxed, so I could enjoy every moment of the performance. Blossom slide off the bed, eased towards to me, leaned over and whispered in my ear, audible enough for Shante to hear, "Thank you for the pleasure of pleasing you.", before easing back into the bed with the helping hand of Shante.

This was going to be a night to remember!

I was still off balance from my first reaction to witnessing Shante nude. I gasped for air when she turned to Blossom for a taste and I witnessed the magnificent display of her moist hairy haven secreting cream. Blossom and I were going to be pioneers tonight, in the pursuit of ecstasy. The only exploration remaining was to experience the delivery of those exquisite tools. Sexy, coos from between Shante's lips, as Blossom slowly licks the lips resting so nicely between the firm thighs of Shante. I watched them enjoy each other and experiment with technique and toys to grade responses. Shante reached over and grasped my third leg firmly, asking was I as good with it as I was with words and Blossom responded for me saying "better." The memories of that moment in time still brings a smile, as I dictate it one more time to delight your mind.

I am unable to sleep having gone so long without your touch. I keep remembering the feel of you sliding into me for the first time after I have gone without you for a while. I am so warm and wet and you so hard the sensations are overwhelming and radiate throughout my entire body. The taste of you is still fresh on my tongue and I would love to taste you while Shante tastes me and you play with her clit with your fingers and a toy. When she is nice and wet and screaming for a stiff dick you would fuck her and my pussy would ache for you, but I would entertain myself with BOB while I watched the two of you. After you have both rested Shante would return her lips and tongue to my body and I would return the favor, tasting your cum on her pussy everywhere. You watch, growing harder by the second. The taste of you drives me wild and as she climaxes you thrust deep into me over and over again and our bodies shudder under the delight of our reunion. I taste you afterwards, enjoying the special mix of our juices running down your shaft.

Shit! I can't write anymore or I will explode. My nipples are so hard and my clit is calling for you. I am so wet that I can feel the juices dripping onto my thighs. I need you to fuck me right now! I would scream your name over and over again until you cum deep inside me. Fuck me! Why have you done this to me? Made me want you so and not be able to have you. Close your eyes and watch me now as I lick my nipples and massage my clit using my juices to glide my finger across the tip of my clit before I plunge my fingers into this wet oasis that is yours. Can you smell my aroma now? Thank you for the pleasure of pleasing you. More later...

FEMININE FLOW OF LIFE

"When two people find each other what should keep them from being together?"

I roll over, to gaze into your eyes and behold the exquisite beauty of your presence. Like a whisper, humming in the afterglow of masculine prowess pleasure pleasing, I am feminine in the infinite flow of illuminating life impregnating energy. It is revitalizing to be free of pretense and liberating to receive pure in your reciprocation. I touch the tip of your nose and you smile. We are purged of all impurities, with a dream of doing the same for so many others in the message we leave here. In our archaic modern society conditioning we carve a character of pretense through statements life "fake it to you make it", until we are oblivious to honesty. The performance becomes reality and defines truth. We cloth ourselves with nudity in fear of our soul becoming totally exposed. The distraction of lust for our physical form influences the mind to neglect its purpose in the flow of life. Our loss of faith in the omnipresence of The Divine influences you to dismiss the role that is mine. I am the camel you forget to bind.

I understand the many forces, some noble in proclamation, designed to distort our natural synergy of compatibility. The whiff of passion lingering in my heart and fragrance of my aura is through the love of you, an amazing woman I adore. Your willingness to love me unconditionally pure is the condition we signed, forged the man I am. I am truly thankful and will always be grateful for you, embracing my role as a beacon in your life. The consideration I leave behind, orated to muse your mind, is the acceptance that who we are is what we attract and what we attract is who we are. Of course, I am not talking about casual or professional relationships, but those relationships that are the most intimate in our life. It is not about blaming or praising yourself, but always examining your life to emerge as better. The way and why I seduce has tamed, while my way and why of romance still remains, as my passion continues the flame. Dress as you dare, bare, rare or with flare for the soul that intrinsically cares. I have lived the life and now I must focus on building a life. In my reasoning, building a life is focused on passing the wisdom of my experiences forward in a form that can be appreciated by the most people. I advise you to look closer at the message in my words, if you have reached this far in my prose and have not discovered the gem forged specifically for you. It is here, for you, I promise. We each must take the risk necessary in offering the greatest benefit possible. It is often in the vibrations of the air to be the change you desire, without asking you to consider what is stimulating those desires defined as yours.

I ponder the fantasy of learning from my experiences in my youthful folly, to shun the trajectory of who I am, only to realize I am. The passion reciprocated, never imagined beforehand, is our genuine vibration of seduction and bathed in romance. It is my effort to established a pattern of being more of a man without simultaneously becoming more male. It is critical important for me to view life from more perspectives than mine to design a better perspective in my service of worship. At first glance, bringing all this together in one prose, will pose a conflict in our conditioning of what we believe is right. In this walk, thought life, I have been erased as a voice and deleted from the footnotes. The way we love self is embedded in every intimate relationship we form and especially in the ones we nurture. Al-Islam is a holistic health way of life and the Originator of Creation is never shy of the truth, no matter how disturbing it will be to you.

MAJESTIC COOING CHARM

Oh! My Cherry Blossom blooming with
enduring love and fabolicious
sexuality

Your Valrhona chocolate charming
ambiance is vibrantly amazing and
irresistibly delightful

An Essence offering one thousand nine
hundred seventy-two years of
tantalizing perfection

Like the exquisite taste of Crème
Brulee' your treat liquefies from the
warmth of my mouth

With an intelligent heart full of exotic
happiness, massaging splendor, you are
absolutely sensational

Pleasures nurtured through seven
months of precious
cultivation exemplifies your beauty

An alluring karma of seven elevations
flourishing graceful harmony and ten
degrees of insightful wisdom you glow
with possibilities

Yum! Yum! Like the purple passion
asparagus standing erect, full of
creamy life, I await your lips

The burgundy color of blood rushes
forth, seeking to satisfy your
yearning, illuminating the room with
intensity and wetness

Wow! Your body and soul is a
sculpture of spirituality and royalty
seeking me for completion

*For seventeen days the orgasmic
cravings and aphrodisiac of your sexy
eyes calling my name stimulates
adventurous desire*

*Oh! Yum! Wow! My blooming Cherry
Blossom I am yours and you are mine*

Figure 6 Algo-rhythmic by Nettrice Gaskin, Ph.D